Make Your

Mess

Your
Memoir

Anna David

ISBN-13: 978-1-951407-21-6 (ebook)
          978-1-951407-22-3 (paperback)

For anyone who's made a mess and has a message

Access the links in this book by
scanning the below QR code.

Table of Contents

Author's Note

I WROTE THIS BOOK FOR a number of reasons. But here's the most relevant one for you: what I've learned about how a book can build a business can change your life.

It wasn't easy to learn any of this. I spent years publishing books the traditional way, having to borrow money because the book advances kept me living just above the poverty level. But by getting out of the traditional publishing game and then discovering the methods I explain in the last quarter of this book, I was able to go from starving artist to thriving business owner.

The clients who have hired my company Launch Pad have been able to use these same techniques—and they've had similar results.

You can, too.

And that brings me back to my reason for writing this book: the ideas, advice, strategies and methodology encapsulated here shouldn't only be for our high-end clients or those who've spent decades in publishing. I want anyone who has the desire to write books and make a living the tools they need to do that.

After reading this book, you might want to contact us to explore how we can help you transform your mess into a message and then a book that builds or creates your business. And that would be delightful! But if you read and absorb everything in here, you may not need to because you may have everything you need.

(If you want to skip my personal story and get right to the instruction, I won't be offended…in fact, I'll never know! Just go straight to Chapter 11. But I promise you'll get more out of this if you follow an example first. Plus the fact that I share my messy life may well convince you that you should share yours, too.)

Foreword

I'M USED TO BEING the behind-the-scenes guy.

For years, I've negotiated tens of millions of dollars in marketing deals for clients like Magic Johnson, Hulk Hogan, Dennis Rodman, Chevy Chase and many other iconic celebrities, traveling around the world and always making sure their messages were heard.

But something happened to me. Something that made me want to go from behind-the-scenes to center stage.

I almost died.

I'm not being dramatic. My addiction to opiates was so severe that I was regularly overdosing even while holding together a successful career.

Then, against all odds, I got sober. I found recovery. And in finding recovery, I found myself.

As the years passed, a little voice inside of me would say, "You could help more people than you can possibly imagine if you go public with your story." Finally, when I was 10 years sober, the voice had become an internal scream. I knew I was ready to share my story. I knew I wanted to become a leader in the addiction recovery movement. And I knew the person who could help get me there: Anna David.

Anna isn't just a woman who, in recovery, has become a *New York Times* bestselling author of multiple books. She's someone uniquely qualified to understand the role a mess can play in a message. She knows that we all have struggles and that the best way to overcome them is to share them so we can help other people.

When Anna published my book, I was hoping it would trickle out and help a few people. What happened instead was a Russian River-like torrent of attention. I went from *Cuomo Prime Time* to *Tucker Carlson Tonight*, landing on the world's biggest podcasts, shows, sites and papers. I was offered multiple spokesperson opportunities and close to a dozen speaking engagements the week the book was released.

While I'd had an inkling that a book could help me spread my message, I had no idea just how much. Overnight, I went from being a guy who'd overcome a drug problem to someone being flown across the world to help other people. And even more surprisingly, the book changed the game of my core business.

I wasn't just Darren Prince, sports and celebrity agent. I was Darren Prince, opiate addict turned recovery advocate. In every business interaction, I was a friend simply because I'd put my story down in a book. I wasn't a "suit" anymore.

In *Make Your Mess Your Memoir*, Anna eloquently and humorously tells her own story—the way she was able to go from struggling addict to successful businesswoman. Then, through a series of instructional chapters, she shows how anyone can take those incidents that have caused them the most shame or taught them the greatest lessons and make that into a message. She even shares ideas for how to use that message to build up a business.

There's no better guidebook that exists when it comes to showing people how to make their tests into their testimony —and then use that as a business tool. And there's no better guide than Anna. Let her teach you what I'm so grateful she taught me.

—Darren Prince, #1 international bestselling author of *Aiming High: How a Prominent Sports Agent Hit Bottom at the Top*

Introduction

BEING STUCK IN AN elevator sucks.

Of course, that's obvious. If we're in an elevator, we're on our way somewhere. And even if that somewhere is home, we have a schedule we're trying to keep and being stuck is stopping us from keeping it.

But there's something worse going on in that elevator, and it's not just the fat, sweaty guy next to us or the crying baby in that woman's arms. It's that I'm-not-here-and-I'm-not-there feeling, that no man's land sensation of being done with where we were, but not quite where we want to be yet. That's then combined with the back-of-the-mind thought... *What if I'm here forever?*

We may not be conscious of it, but that comforting tug when the elevator kicks back into gear and we know we're not stuck anymore is as much a relief that we're getting away from the sweaty guy as it is a relief that we won't forever be, like John Cusack in *Being John Malkovich*, stuck between the seventh and eighth floors.

Don't believe me? Think about your biggest struggle, the one you maybe want to write a book about.

My guess is that it had three stages—denial, awareness and solution. And it was the middle one—the stuck-in-the-elevator phase—that really sucked.

Denial, frankly, isn't so bad. There's a reason "ignorance is bliss" is a cliché. But awareness? Oh, what a rude awakening

—especially when you realize *you* are the problem…that you are doing something that is hurting you or others and yet you are somehow powerless to stop. This is when the elevator is indeed stuck between the seventh and eighth floors. The awareness stage can literally kill you.

Changing who we are and how we behave is incredibly painful but behaving in self-destructive ways is also incredibly painful. It's only when the pain of changing who we are and how we behave outweighs the pain of our self-destructive ways that we'll even consider getting out of our own way.

And that's where the solution comes—not always easily, usually not quickly. But it does.

Of course, you already know this. You know this because you made it to the other side.

And now you want to help reach those people who are sandwiched between the seventh and eighth floors. You want to be that emergency call button. You want to be a part of the relief people feel when the elevator kicks back into gear and they know they're not stuck anymore.

With this book, I'm going to show you how I did that—and how you can, too.

Because here's the deal: 20 years ago, I was a struggling writer who surrounded herself with only cats and cocaine. I couldn't make a living. I thought about killing myself a lot. Then, against all odds, I got sober. The elevator got un-stuck. And once I got out, I couldn't be stopped. I wanted everyone to know what I wished I'd known when I was in stage two—aware but without a solution. I wanted to clarify the misconceptions I'd had about addiction and recovery. I wanted people to know how possible it was to live a different way.

And so I wrote a book about it.

Years later, after much struggle, I was a *New York Times* bestselling author of a bunch of books about addiction and recovery. I was giving TEDx talks, touring colleges, appearing on *The Today Show, The Talk, The CBS Morning Show* and Fox News.

But just because I was sober and out there doesn't mean I was entirely un-stuck. I spent years trying to make a living as a traditionally published author and website editor. I spent years accepting the unacceptable, both personally and professionally.

Push forward. Try harder. Make. It. Work. No matter how you're treated.

It was only when I stopped trying to make my life look the way I thought it should that I could build a life I loved. And one of the reasons I love it is that it includes helping other people share their stories.

Why does this matter? Because I grew up feeling un-seen, un-heard and ashamed. And I don't want anyone else to feel that way. If you have a story to share, God damn it, I want people to hear and see you share it. I want this not only so you can relish in your glorious you-ness but also so you can release any shame you may be holding onto, since sharing is the greatest shame eradicator I know of. So I'm telling you about my struggles and how they led to my freedom, because I want you to know that this can be true for you, too.

In the first part of the book, I'm going to walk you through my journey—the early life that set me up to want to escape, the recovery that provided me with some footing, the struggles that followed as I tried to find my career and personal path and finally, how I was able to make that mess into my message.

In the second part, I'm going to show you how you can make your own mess into your message. Because it's a combination of a memoir and a business book—and because mem-biz would sound, frankly, terrible —I'm creating a new genre I'm calling *biz-oir*.

Here's why I've done it this way: we're all being pummeled with thousands of ideas and thoughts every day. Our attention span is allegedly eight seconds long. So how do we retain anything? There's a simple answer: story. It's how memory experts teach people to remember.

In other words, by sharing my story before telling you the most effective way I know for you to share yours, I'm hoping you'll be able to use what I've done as a model.

The first part—the memoir section—follows the structure I used for my *New York Times* bestselling book; it's also the one we use for the books we publish at Launch Pad. I delve into that structure in detail in part two, and I've also distilled into a one-page cheat sheet you can get by going to www.messdownload.com. In fact, I highly recommend grabbing it now.

Are you back? Good. Because now I'm going to tell you my story.

Then I'm going to tell you how you can make your own mess into your message. And then into your memoir.

So let's get into it.

PART 1
THE MESS

CHAPTER 1

Yes, I *Am* an Author

"YOU WROTE A BOOK?" he asked, his eyes boring into mine.

I nodded. We were sitting under the bright studio lights of a TV studio in midtown Manhattan where I seemed to be blowing the show host's mind. We were talking about Paris Hilton going to jail or flashing paparazzi or maybe it was Lindsay Lohan going to jail—I honestly did so many of those segments back then that they all blended together.

During the segment, I mentioned that my book, *Party Girl*, was about addiction and recovery and that Paris and Lindsay may be suffering from substance abuse issues.

After the taping, the show host found me in the green room and asked me if I could come back on the show—not to talk about a celebrity but to discuss me and my book.

I'd been appearing on TV for a few years by then. It had started accidentally, when a CNN show had needed someone who worked at an entertainment magazine to discuss a celebrity and I'd been available. I agreed, it went well and that's when I found myself appearing regularly on *The Today Show*, *The Talk*, *The CBS Morning Show* and the like.

But I was perfectly clear about my role: Paris Hilton and Lindsay Lohan attracted viewers. Paris Hilton and Lindsay Lohan would not come on *The Today Show*, Fox News or CNN to discuss their party girl antics. But I would. So those shows could cover Hilton or Lohan without needing to bother with publicists and negotiations and hearing no.

I understood that those shows didn't care about *me*.

But then suddenly they did.

Yes, my book, the one I'd started on a whim at my friend Melanie's kitchen table, had gotten one of the biggest news show hosts in the world to want to devote an episode to me. We scheduled a time for me to come back a few weeks later and, as promised, we did a segment all about me and my book.

That's when I truly learned the power of having the word "author" associated with my name.

But that wasn't the only surprise of the trip. When I got back to my hotel that night, my agent called and told me that we were in the midst of a bidding war over the *Party Girl* film rights. A mother-daughter producing duo wanted to make it into a Lifetime movie, an independent producer wanted to make it as an indie movie and Melanie Griffith wanted to make it into a mainstream movie with me as the writer.

After that, there was an onslaught of publicity for my book—I discussed it on a slew of CNN, NBC and CBS shows and it started getting written about in publications like *Cosmo, The New York Daily News* and *Redbook*, among others. This meant that I was suddenly receiving hundreds of messages from people all over the world who were struggling with addiction. I had inadvertently walked into a situation where I could help a lot of people.

That was a decade and a half ago. Every year since, I've become all the more able to embrace my mess and crystalize my message. At nearly 20 years of sobriety, more of my puzzle pieces fit together than they did back then. Who knows, in another 20 years, I may even have the whole puzzle finished.

But for now, all I can do is go back to the beginning to trace how this whole mess started.

CHAPTER 2

My New Personality

"**I** LIKE JANE," MY MOM SAID. "She's so effervescent."

I nodded. I liked Jane, too. And although, at the age of 12, I didn't know what the word *effervescent* meant, I loved the sound of it. It made me think of bubbles and excitement.

I told Mom that from then on, I wanted to be effervescent, too.

***

We were on a cruise to Alaska with my entire family—and when I say *entire* family, I'm talking grandfather, his wife, his kids, his kids' kids (me, my brother, my two cousins), his wife's kids and their kids. It was my grandfather's 80th birthday and he was celebrating by taking us all on this cruise.

My grandfather had a lot of money.

Money was an extremely confusing thing to me growing up because there seemed to be so much conversation about its importance but it never seemed to make anyone happy.

Take my grandfather, for instance: he'd brought all of us on this extravagant family cruise but in the dining room where we ate breakfast, lunch and dinner over the course of those two weeks, he sat at a table with my grandmother while the other adults sat at another table and my brother, cousins and I made up the children's table.

He'd paid for all of us to come on this cruise, in other words, but he didn't speak to any of us.

That was actually fine with me because I found my grandfather terrifying. My mom's dad had died before I was born so this was the only real, live example I had of a grandfather and he was nothing like the ones in the Country Time Lemonade commercials.

My grandfather didn't sit on a porch or tell me I was the apple of his eye. He told me I was stupid. All the time. When he taught me to play Gin Rummy and I immediately beat him, he turned bright red, started banging on the table and then pushed all the cards onto the ground.

"There's no way you could beat me!" he raged. "This is ridiculous!"

I was shaking. Why oh why oh why hadn't I just let him win?

Then he seemed to calm down.

"I'm not upset that you beat me," he clarified. "I'm upset because you didn't do it with strategy. You got lucky. And that's lazy. You shouldn't be so stupid."

Anyway, that was Grandpa. His third wife, while not horrible per se, didn't do anything to stop him from raging against children or anyone else. I hated going to visit them in Palm Springs but somehow I was always being sent down there, alone. My brother was much better than me at ducking out of things.

Let's just say I was thrilled to be at the kid's table on that trip.

***

"Oh my God, it was so good," Jane said when she found me by the ping pong table one afternoon at the end of the first week of the cruise. She ran her hands through her curly blond hair dramatically as she sat down next to me.

She had just been to see *Sophie's Choice* in the cruise ship movie theater and was telling me how it had "torn her heart out." I was listening to her but mostly I was admiring how confidently she was expressing her sadness. She really seemed to own how important her feelings were, how much they mattered, how necessary they were to express. I marveled at this.

I asked her to tell me the plot and when she did, I was even more impressed. This was a deep movie! Jane cared about important things! She was one year older than me and, in addition to all her other virtues, deeply wise.

As we talked, we started hitting the ping pong ball back and forth. I had gotten pretty good at ping pong during this trip. Never athletic, I'd successfully avoided sports for most of my life. When, in sixth grade, we started playing dodgeball every Friday during PE, I'd have my mom write a note saying I was sick and would have to sit out. Every Friday, I stood against the wall and clutched my stomach, convincingly playing the part of the sick kid as pubescent boys hurled balls at my friends' faces.

But ping pong wasn't pubescent boys hurling balls at my face. Ping pong wasn't tennis either. My parents had sent me to tennis camp and I just...sucked. The jury was in: I was not athletic. And this was a major bummer since it was becoming increasingly clear to me that being athletic was a crucial aspect of being popular.

Popularity was as confusing to me as money.

From kindergarten on, I made friends easily and learned to navigate social situations well. But I was not athletic. And no matter how good you were socially, it was hard to bounce back from being picked last for sports teams.

Also, apparently I was shy.

I learned this accidentally one day, when I heard my mom describe me as "shy, like her father." My ears perked up in horror. I was SHY? I didn't want to be shy! While I couldn't control my lack of athletic ability, I could do something about the shyness.

Jane was my Sherpa.

During that trip, I learned to effervesce by osmosis.

One day, at "bouillon," which was a daily meal on this cruise (cruises serve roughly 80,000 meals a day), Jane and I met two boys—Kevin and John. They were also 12 and 13. She liked John. John liked her. Kevin liked me. And so I, of course, liked Kevin.

What this means, I have no idea. It was all very innocent. I think it just meant we played doubles ping pong and then I would go off with Kevin and she would go off with John and we would all have the sort of deep, meaningful conversations 12-year-olds have?

No idea.

I do remember that Kevin gave me a very sweet goodbye letter the day the cruise ended, along with some maple candy that I never ate—either because it felt too meaningful to consume or because maple candy just doesn't taste good or both.

***

The following winter, I stood at the top of a Squaw Valley ski run.

"You can do it," my dad said.

But his tone wasn't encouraging.

His tone said: You have to do it.

Freezing and on the verge of tears, I watched a kid I knew from math class squeal with joy as he pushed off the mountain and tackled one enormous mogul after another, his skis slicing into the mountain as he continued to holler with joy.

I started to cry.

"Oh, come on," my dad said.

That only made me cry harder.

But I understood the situation. I was at the top. At the bottom, there was warmth and hot chocolate and no scary ice patches that could kill me if my skis happened to slide against them at the wrong angle.

I had to get down.

That's when my dad started laughing.

My family always laughed at me for being so sensitive. I longed to be tough—or at least to be able to ignore my feelings or push them down the way they seemed to. But it never worked.

The day before, on the drive to Tahoe, I'd started crying because I felt like they were being mean to me. I felt like that a lot.

"Oh, my little actress," my dad said, referring to me in the third person, the way he always did when he teased me. He caught my eye in the rear-view mirror. "She's so good at crying when she wants something."

This, of course, only made me cry harder.

I wanted them to stop being mean to me. I wanted to be like Jane. Sure, she cried when she watched *Sophie's Choice* but her crying indicated strength; she was together enough to cry over Meryl Streep's fictional choices. She didn't cry out of weakness.

As my crying turned to full blown sobs, I heard the sound.

It was a terrible sound—one of the worst I'd ever known.

It was my dad's cackle.

It wasn't a laugh. It never came out when something was actually funny. It was a laugh that said, "You are being ridiculous and everyone knows it."

And then...the second worse sound in the world: my mom laughing. I understood, even then, why she did it. There was often a strained anxiety in the air—silence or stress—when my dad was around and my dad's cackle was a rare respite, a sign that happy times might be coming.

My mom's laugh wasn't as cruel as my dad's. But as I listened to their laughter, I felt like they each had a hand on either side of my heart and they were twisting it, the way I sometimes twisted a towel to dry it.

That's when my brother joined in. His laugh seemed to say: it's nice to see my parents enjoying each other for once; why not join in?

We drove.

A light snow fell.

They laughed.

I cried.

At the top of the mountain, I reminded myself that getting down this slope was actually easier than being in that car.

And so I took a deep breath, shifted my skis the way I'd learned to do in the Squaw Valley Kids Ski School and pushed forward.

And then I fell.

I got up, tried again, fell again.

"Don't cry, don't cry," I ordered myself before falling again.

And that's when I fell yet again. I took off my skis and walked the rest of the way down.

My dad was still laughing.

***

I was much better on my own two feet. In fact, when it didn't have to do with sports, I was one of the most ambitious kids in the world.

I looked at *The Guinness Book of World Records* almost every day, tracing my hands over the picture of the tallest man (he was standing next to a street sign that was dwarfed by his presence), the fattest twins (they were on motorcycles and wore cowboy hats) and the youngest author (she was six and looked very pleased with herself while leaning back on a white fence).

My obsession with world records only grew when Cindy and Bobby Brady tried to set the world's teeter totter record on *The Brady Bunch*. While they had given up before actually setting the record, that was a moot point as far as I was concerned; the local paper had come out and taken their photo. And their family was so proud!

I think that was the part that impacted me the most. Setting a record, assuming it wasn't a record related to being fat or tall, seemed to embody everything that mattered: it showed that you were the best, it made everyone support you and it brought you a measure of fame.

And so, one summer day, I asked my mom to drive me to my friend Ramsay's so we could set the world record for longest time on a swing set.

Ramsay's house was in Sausalito, next door to a park that always seemed to be empty. Ramsay was, like Jane, fearless. When I called to tell her I'd be there in half an hour, wearing the shiny velour jacket we both had and that she should wear hers too, she agreed and said she'd call the local paper to let them know a record was going to be set and they should come cover it.

By this point, I'd not only learned what the word effervescent meant but I'd also really managed to become it. I don't know whether it was the simple act of making a decision to be different after meeting Jane or if my childhood shyness was just a phase, but no one thought I was shy anymore.

Still, none of my ambitious plans were particularly well thought-out. Ramsay and I, for instance, hadn't spent a lot of time planning this out or doing any research on, say, what the current record for time spent on a swing set was. We just went in with a sort of blind faith that we would somehow surpass it.

It was the same with my other projects. The week before, I'd gotten very excited about gathering signatures for a petition. But it wasn't to help animals, a local politician or some other cause that I was passionately connected to. I just liked a project. That project had been inspired by the fact that one day, at United Market, the cashier had informed my mom that they were considering no longer allowing people to pay by check.

My friend Katy was with me when the cashier gave my

mom the news and Katy agreed with me that this was outrageous. Surely, we figured, the rest of the community would be up in arms about this concept?

And so Katy and I created a petition and stood outside United Market asking people to sign it. We were very impassioned, but most of the people we spoke to didn't seem to understand why this potential policy not to take checks was so pertinent.

We came home with one signature, given to us by a woman who probably pitied us.

Katy was also my primary co-producer in the shows I liked to put on and perform in. Our productions were simple. I would usually lip sync a song from *Chorus Line* and then we would choreograph a dance or two and Katy would recite a monologue or play. Still, we took them very seriously—rehearsing for hours, creating programs and telling each other we were making something extremely special that was possibly going to transform the world.

While we'd occasionally attempt to go wide by inviting neighbors to come, selling tickets and even bags of popcorn, usually it was just an audience made up of our moms.

But that day on the Sausalito swing set, Ramsay and I didn't have an audience. No one clapped for us. The reporter from the local paper never came. By the third hour, we were bored and tired and just decided to stop.

Then we went into her house in our matching shiny jackets to watch *The Brady Bunch*.

CHAPTER 3

You-Know-Who

YOU ALWAYS REMEMBER YOUR first time.

I know this because I've sat in 12-step meetings with hundreds of strangers over the years and I've heard more of them than I can even count describe the first time they drank with more detail than they can describe what they did the day before.

My first time actually wasn't that remarkable.

I was 12 years old and my friend Maria had made the plan: we would chug vodka from her mother's liquor cabinet, fill the bottle back with water and then take the bus into the city to meet two boys from our eighth grade class.

My excitement over this plan diminished when it became a reality. The vodka burned going down and when we got to the city and sat on cloudy Baker Beach with Charlie and Ethan, drinking more, Charlie leaned over and casually vomited over his shoulder.

"Carrots," he remarked, shrugging before taking another chug.

The jury was in: drinking was gross.

If only I'd left it there.

But no, a few months later, I was with a different group of friends one night in a park in Fairfax.

People were passing around beer.

This was different from vodka; it was oddly delicious. It felt so good going down my throat, like a peaceful river and not like the wild torrent vodka had been.

And what it *did* to me?

I was effervescent, without having to exert even the slightest bit of effort. It was like every voice that had ever stopped me from being my very best self was erased and every voice that told me I was amazing got put on high volume. I was funny and charming and attractive and the chatter that I didn't even consciously realize was always in my head evaporated.

What did we talk about that night? No idea. All I remember is that someone there knew Alison, my favorite babysitter from when I was a kid.

I sat on that park bench, talking to that guy, buzzed, remembering how Alison had made me an R2D2 costume when I was eight. Even though *Star Wars* had been my brother's thing and really the only reason I was R2D2 was that he had wanted to be C3P0 and I had to be something that fit with that, Alison made our costumes with so much love that I no longer cared about how I thought *Star Wars* was stupid and overrated and boring.

That's how alcohol felt to me then—like a babysitter who loved me so much that she could make something stupid and overrated and boring feel amazing.

***

My love affair with alcohol moved to the next stage the night I went to my first high school party.

I was a freshman and this party was at a senior boy's house so I was both deeply impressed with myself for finding out about it as well as anxious as could be. But after quickly downing two beers, that anxious girl drifted into the ether and Effervescent Anna began to shine.

Effervescent Anna didn't let an opportunity slip her by. And so, when Mike Goldberg, the senior boy widely considered to be God's Gift to Womankind, walked by, I touched his arm.

"I have 'Anna + Mike' and a heart circled around it on my binder," I told him by way of introduction. Then I added, "I'm Anna."

While Mike was obviously aware of his King of the School status, I had ignored Cool Rule #1: *Cool people do not acknowledge the superior among us.* Drawing "Anna + Mike" with a heart around it on my binder was one thing but *telling him that I had?*

Potential social suicide!

But that's the thing about Effervescent Anna: she didn't care. And Cool Rule #2 is *Don't care.*

Or at least that's what I concluded when Mike looked bemused—and charmed. "I have the same thing on my binder," he finally said. And then he gave me that crinkly-eyed smile that had earned him his God-like status. "You're cute," he added, before a succession of fans descended upon him.

And that's when I understood: alcohol could not only make me into whoever I wanted to be. It could also get me whatever I wanted to have.

***

"Anna, can you come out here, please?" My mom stood at my bedroom door, a strained look on her face.

I looked up from my French homework, panicked; what had I done? And then I realized: my dad was home and since he usually came home after I was asleep, something had to be amiss. I was definitely in trouble.

But for what?

Had they figured out that when I'd said Katy's dad had taken us to a movie last Friday night, Katy, Tanya and I had actually been drinking in Katy's older brother's music studio?

Had Katy's dad called?

I tried to remain calm as my mom led me to where my dad sat in a chair by the fireplace, a gin and tonic and can of Beer Nuts on the table next to him.

But this time my parents were presenting a united front. They weren't laughing at me, though. What was going on?

"Something's going to be in the paper tomorrow," my dad finally said.

Relief shot through me. This couldn't have to do with me. I nodded, slowly, still not entirely sure I was in the clear.

"Something...about you?" I asked.

He nodded.

My dad was quite well-known in the Bay Area. He owned an electronics store and a computer store and he'd started the electronics store, Matthews, with a $3000 loan from his mother. It was now a multi-million-dollar business that advertised on the radio and local TV non-stop.

As a kid, I had loved it. I would get on the school bus or be in a store and his commercials would be playing on the radio; no matter where I was, I could hear my dad's voice talking about the deals they offered at "the top of the hill, Daly City." I was proud of what he had accomplished and how everyone seemed to know who he was.

Even when people called him "The Crazy Eddie of the West Coast," I was proud. Better to be somebody than nobody, I figured.

But this level of pseudo-fame, he was explaining, came at a price.

"I did something that any smart businessman would do," he explained. He paused, grabbed some nuts, threw them in his mouth. "They've decided to make an example out of me because they knew it would make news. It was really just a misunderstanding."

I nodded, waiting for more.

Silence.

I didn't ask who "they" were or what he had done.

"Just so you know," he said. My mom looked down.

It was clear that the conversation was over. I just had no idea what it meant.

***

I learned more the next day, when *The San Francisco Chronicle*'s story came out and wrote about what he'd done.

I didn't really understand the details of the *Chronicle* story, or what my dad had done; I believed him when he said it was a misunderstanding and hoped no one would care about the incident at all. I reminded myself that Michelle Dawson's dad had been caught up in a big embezzlement scandal the year before and she hadn't become any sort of a social pariah.

I did wish my brother wasn't away at boarding school. Michelle Dawson had a sister and brother who all went to our school. At least they hadn't had to walk down the long stairway from the parking lot to the main campus all alone.

But the entire morning passed without anyone saying a word to me about the story, so I just told myself that no one had read it.

But then it happened.

I remember exactly where I was standing when Taylor Parsons came up to me—near the pay phone outside of French class.

"Hi Anna!" she said. She wore a sickly sweet smile as she walked toward me. Then she reached an arm out and patted my shoulder. "I want you to know I'm here if you need anything."

I nodded, shame shooting through me. Effervescent Anna was gone. I picked at my cuticles.

I hated Taylor in that moment, hated her pity and the fact that she was doing "the right thing." I hated that I was someone for whom *anyone* had to do the right thing.

Although we weren't friends, our friend groups were adjacent. She was in the "good girl" group—the group between cool and nerdy—while I was desperately clinging to the cool group. Taylor and her friends were sweet. They were friends with all the same boys my friends were friends with, but they didn't date them. They went to the same parties but they didn't drink.

Still, I knew that Taylor had been put up to this conversation by her mom.

Everyone knew Taylor's mom.

She was the quintessential Marin do-everything-right-but-talk-so-much-shit-behind-your-back mom. She was on all the boards, always donating things to the school and showboating her generosity. To look at this woman's face was to know that she reveled in the misfortunes of others; the woman feasted on pity.

"Do you know what's going to happen?" Taylor asked, and I realized she hadn't just been sent on this task to show me how good she and her family were; she was there to dig for dirt.

"It's all fine," I finally said.

We both knew she couldn't help. What was she going to do? Take my dad's actions back? Make me not feel like I was waiting for some pronouncement that I was no longer accepted?

Why, I asked myself as I continued walking to French class, couldn't she have had the decency to ignore this whole mess like everyone else?

***

After that, things changed. I went from being a part of things to being on the outskirts. Even though my dad didn't end up going to jail, most people seemed to think that he did.

I would still sometimes be invited to the right parties, but only as an afterthought. The main events that my so-called friends were putting together excluded me.

There were several actions I could have taken. I could have transferred to a less snobby and far larger school where no one cared that your dad was on the front page of the paper over a misunderstanding.

Or, even simpler, I could have befriended the uncool girls—the heavier ones who loved history class and didn't kiss boys or go to parties. Taylor's group was out of the question:

sanctimonious do-good-ing was never my vibe.

I chose, instead, to cling to my crowd.

I chose, in other words, to put myself in situation after situation where I was either barely invited or not invited.

At the end of junior year, thumbing through my friend Diana's yearbook, I read an inscription from the cruelest of these "friends." *We had so many great times this year,* Cory Carlson wrote in that curly cursive so popular among adolescents. Then below that, as a parenthetical: *(except when you-know-who invited herself along)*.

Reading something like that and knowing that *you're* the you-know-who is an experience I wouldn't wish on any teenage girl.

It's no wonder my relationship with alcohol grew. It's also no wonder that you-know-who couldn't wait to get to college.

CHAPTER 4

Person-to-Person Call for Professor Newton

"PERSON-TO-PERSON CALL for Professor Newton," Chris said into the phone. "Do you accept?"

"I do," Professor Newton, our math professor, responded.

Chris grinned, pressed the receiver button down and dialed our friend Jason's number. Lowering his voice, he said, "Person-to-person call for Jason. Do you accept?"

"Sure," Jason said, sounding a bit apprehensive.

Chris then put the conversation on speaker and muted our side. He, Jamie and I sat on my bed, clutching each other, already in hysterics.

And then we listened to our math professor—the oddest man I'd ever met, a person who managed to make calculus more confusing with every class and who gave most of his students D's—talk to our friend Jason. Chris and I silently howled as we listened to them trying to figure out why the other had called them.

It was a genius trick. Chris had first broken it down for me the week before, explaining that the phones in our dorms allowed you to connect one call to another.

It was his idea to call up one person, pretend to be an operator placing a "person-to-person" call and then call a person we knew they would have an incredibly awkward conversation with, pretend to be that same operator…and voila! You have two people who would have an uncomfortable conversation even if they *had* actually meant to call one another each thinking the other had called them and spending the whole phone call trying to figure out why. And we got to listen to the whole thing!

We thought it was hilarious.

And actually, it *was* hilarious.

Because we'd already done this to Jason the previous week— connecting him in a "person-to-person" call with Sandra, my next-door neighbor in the dorms who we knew had a wicked crush on him—the math teacher call only lasted a minute.

"Um, sorry, Professor Newton, I think Chris and Anna are playing a joke," Jason said after Professor Newton asked why he was calling. Chris, Jamie and I collapsed in laughter and then started to count to 10. At nine, Jason knocked on my dorm room door.

"Very funny guys," he said. "You trying to get me a D minus?"

The person-to-person call trick was one of several schemes Chris, Jamie and I came up with. It was hilarious and delightful. And really, that was my freshman year of college.

College was a revelation. There I was in Connecticut, 3000 miles from my family and my so-called high school friends. Finally, I was among my people.

Trinity College is what is known as a "little ivy." What

that really means is that it's full of a bunch of kids who went to Exeter, Andover and all the fanciest prep schools, but were too busy having fun to get into the colleges they were supposed to attend, like Harvard or Yale. They were the spoiled, beautiful, fun kids...smart enough to skate by but with social priorities far above academic ones.

I felt like I could finally exhale.

I was from a family that prioritized academics. My father had gone to Harvard. His mother had gone to Radcliffe. My dad's dad, while not great at gin rummy, had gone to Yale Law School.

My high school prided itself on being rigorous academically. What that actually meant is that nothing mattered more than getting A's and high SAT scores, even if the A's were procured by cheating and the SAT scores by figuring out the systems that could strategically earn you the best score.

I know this because my dad sent me to three different SAT tutors every time my disappointing test scores came in. I eventually ended up being tutored by a guy who'd written all the biggest books about how to game the SAT.

Even though he taught me all the tricks to rig those standardized tests, I still never got the scores my family wanted.

I understood why, though.

Growing up, one thing had been hammered home to me again and again: my brother was smart and I was pretty. In other words, I was not smart. While we both applied to Harvard, he was accepted and I was not. (I later found out that my dad and grandfather called in a favor to get him in and did not do that for me.)

Still, I was fairly convinced by that point in life—even

though I got decent grades—that I was all but a raving idiot.

At Trinity I didn't feel like an idiot. I felt like I was surrounded by a lot of smart, cool people and I fit right in.

Basically, I was at a college with a great reputation for academics but that also had a Halloween party which had made a *Playboy* magazine list of best college parties. It was a place where it was acceptable to drink every night of the week, as well as during the day on weekends.

In recovery, we talk about when drinking "really worked." Boy oh boy did drinking work for me at Trinity.

When Chris, Jamie and I weren't pulling off hijinks that everyone seemed to find hilarious, even when the joke was on them, we were either drinking, planning our drinking or getting over our drinking.

Oh, we also went to class. But after a rigorous childhood and adolescence made up of classes followed by ballet followed by play rehearsals followed by homework, I marveled at how much freedom I had. Once my classes were over—usually around 1 pm—I could do whatever I wanted.

And there were boys—amazing boys—everywhere. Tossing footballs on the quad. Playing beer pong in their fraternities. On the floor below me in my dorm. And they gave me so much attention! While I'd been popular with boys in grammar school, the ones at my high school only seemed to care about going to Grateful Dead shows and getting high while watching the sunset at the Headlands. At Trinity, I wasn't scrambling to keep up and be a part of; I was leading the way.

Life had never felt so sweet. No one knew or cared about who my dad was. I was just Anna, exotic simply by virtue of the fact that I was from California, naturally effervescent and finally free.

There were no Cory Carlsons at Trinity. The focus wasn't on ostracizing people. We were all united in our goal: to have a good time.

***

"Want a line?" Sean asked me, pushing a small mirror my way. I'd been pretending that I hadn't noticed he was doing cocaine.

I had first tried cocaine in high school and loved it. But I loved it in the way you love eating the entire s'mores cake one night, telling yourself you're disgusting as you lick marshmallows and chocolate off your fingers. In other words, I loved it because it was such an insanely decadent, unusual, outrageous thing to do.

But over the years, my stance shifted.

Cocaine is like that crush on the sixth year senior, the one who should have graduated but is still hanging around and is never going to do anything with his life. You try to ignore him because you know he's a loser but you can't. He looks at you from across the table and you want to tell him to stop staring but instead you find yourself looking back and then getting that uncomfortable twinge of excitement when your eyes connect.

In other words, I'd started seeking it out.

After years of partying around the same people, you learn which are the ones who do drugs. Sean's dad was a famous novelist and he lived in an off-campus apartment filled with real furniture that made our tapestries and Robert Doisneau *Kiss by the Hotel de Ville* posters seem so very "college." He also always had cocaine.

And that's the reason I said yes when he invited me and my friends over.

Still, I acted surprised by the cocaine offer and then pretended to have to think about it.

Slowly shrugging, I finally said, "Why not?" I'm not sure who I was acting for.

The second I did that line, I wanted another. And another. And another. But still playing the part of the girl who only agrees to do drugs because they're in front of her, I waited patiently—by which I mean picking at my cuticles until they bled—for Sean to pass the mirror my way again.

***

"I think something's wrong," I said to my boyfriend Scott as he snored. Then I shook him awake and said it louder.

He shot up in bed. And just as quickly, I jumped out of bed and ran to his bathroom, where I threw up. He followed me, doing exactly what a guy like him does: wet a hand towel, put it on my forehead and then sit with me as I continued to vomit.

The casual few lines I'd intended to do at Sean's had turned into an all-out bender, something I'd attempted to hide from Scott when I met up with him later at his fraternity. Scott and I drank together—all the time—but he was anti-drugs. The minute he told me that, a week or two into our relationship, I knew I would have to lie to him if I ever did coke.

Lying wasn't the only bad thing I did in that relationship.

Frankly, I was a nightmare to date when I was in college and the more nightmare-ishly I behaved, the more boys seemed to want to date me. I careened from one boyfriend to the next with the same pattern: find a boy, fall for him, date him for six to nine months, meet another boy, be spontaneously crazy for him, make out with him, break up with the current boyfriend and then make the new guy into my new boyfriend for the next six to nine months before continuing the pattern.

I wish I could tell you it felt terrible to behave so selfishly, but it didn't. At the time I simply believed men were mine for the taking and I could pick them up and toss them aside like they were a dress I'd stopped wearing and might take to Goodwill if only I could be bothered to go there.

How desirable, attractive, kind or amazing they were or how good they were to me didn't seem to matter once I set my sights on someone else.

Case in point: I had met Scott at a party when I was dating Matt Damon.

Yes, Matt Damon. The actor. Not just a guy with that name.

I spent a lot of time at Harvard, first because Jamie's best friend from high school went there and later because Jamie and I befriended another guy who later became ambassador to England during the Obama presidency. (Let's just call this whole section one long name drop.)

One weekend when Jamie and I were visiting our friend, I met Matt. I later came to understand how successful he became because, in addition to being incredibly talented, he is also the most determined person I've ever known. Which is to say: when I met him at the beginning of the night, he seemed like a nice enough guy who was kind of cute and was shooting his first movie and by the end of the night, his dogged, endlessly charming determination to woo me was so effective that I felt like I was in love.

Anyway, Matt and I had been very happy, very in love, for nine months. Then…Scott. I met Scott at a party, wasted, and felt like it was love at first sight. We confirmed this by making out all night. The next day, I drove to Harvard to break up with Matt. It was Valentine's Day.

But my callousness wasn't limited to the way I picked up and discarded these boys like they were pieces of tissue. I also tore them apart when I lost my temper. While I now see all of this as unresolved trauma—I had misdirected rage that I blasted onto the people closest to me—at the time I simply excelled at mistreating wonderful men.

This means that when I confessed to Scott in between bouts of vomiting that I'd been doing cocaine all night before I'd met up with him, he only nodded. Hours earlier, he had confronted me about it. "You're being weird," he'd said. "You're not on drugs, right?"

I'd acted incensed. "Don't be ridiculous!" I'd responded, wiping my nose, probably talking a million miles a minute.

But as I lay there on the linoleum floor, so appreciating its coolness on my burning hot forehead, he just got me another cold hand towel and told me he loved me.

***

It was a few months later, roughly nine months into my senior year of college, that it occurred to me that I had absolutely no idea what I was going to do when I graduated.

Despite the fact that I had surely been receiving information for the previous two decades that figuring out your life was crucial, the realization that I hadn't a clue about my future descended upon me randomly and dramatically as I sat smoking cigarettes with my quad mates one winter morning.

"Wait, what are you doing in the fall?" I asked Olivia.

"Moving back to DC with Neal," she said, talking about the boyfriend she ended up marrying. "He's helping me to get a job at a non-profit there."

I was dumbfounded. She'd figured all this out? How had I forgotten to? I looked at Sara.

"I'm starting at Foote Cone and Belding in October," she said. "Going to be the assistant to the woman I interned for last summer."

Now I was even more dumbfounded. Sara and Olivia were so on top of things! But that had to be unusual, I thought. Surely other people were in my situation?

At that point our friend Jeff poked his head into our room to see if we were planning to walk over to the dining hall for breakfast or if we wanted to avoid the cold and just order a pizza with him.

"Jeff, what are you doing in the fall?" I asked him.

"Moving to the city with Steve," he answered. "We're both doing the Morgan Stanley trainee program."

"Does Steve want to come to breakfast?" Sara asked, clearly making the decision that the group of us were going to the dining hall. Jeff nodded. Sara put out her cigarette. Everyone seemed to take it for granted that we all knew exactly where we were going next.

I watched Jamie stand up and grab her coat. I knew that she was also moving to Manhattan with her boyfriend and starting her MFA program in the fall.

How on earth, I wondered, had I missed the announcement that I was supposed be to, um, planning a life?

***

There are the classic anxiety dreams you hear about: you show up for the test and have forgotten to study, you're somehow naked when everyone else is wearing clothes, you walk out onto stage for the play but realize you don't know your lines.

My recurring dream for the 20 years after I graduated from college was this: it's the last day of college and most people have already left. Their rooms have been emptied out, their boxes have been shipped. And I am standing in a room or an apartment or a house that is filled with things—many of them items I've never even seen before—and I can't figure out where to find boxes.

Sometimes, I'm madly calling box stores but discovering they're closed. Sometimes I'm walking through room after room, wondering how I could have accumulated so much stuff and cursing myself for doing that without realizing that it was only going to end up slowing me down.

Occasionally, I would discover cats—either in my pocket or in one of the rooms. And this would only add to my stress. How was I going to get everything packed and out of there right away and also care for these animals?

While those dreams didn't start until after I graduated from college, the feeling started after downing the pancakes, hash browns and eggs with Sara, Olivia, Jamie, Jeff and Steve that morning when I realized college was really ending. Camp Trin Trin was no more. I had to get serious about trying to plan a life.

The problem was, I had no idea what sort of life I wanted to have.

I wanted to scream at the entire dining hall, "Can't we all

just stay here for the rest of our lives, going to football games and on-campus concerts and fraternity parties and occasionally to class?"

No one else seemed to wonder this. No one else seemed to want this.

And so I tried, diligently, to think about the sort of life I wanted to have.

But nothing came to me.

I've never been good at planning the future and in the moment when it seemed most crucial, I could only picture a sort of blank wall where the rest of my life was supposed to be.

I had this vague idea that I wanted to be terribly glamorous and so I would envision myself wearing business casual suits and high heels (two items that, to this day, I have never owned), walking around an office in a city, ordering people to do things.

That was as specific as it got.

Scott was a year behind me in school and I realized then that he had been trying for a few months to instigate conversations with me about our future. He would suggest that I try to get a job at a magazine in New York, which was only an hour from school, for the following year and then, when he graduated, we could move in together.

This sounded…possible. Did it sound good? I couldn't tell.

And so I did what you do when you don't have any other options: I acted as if I wanted to move to New York and work at a magazine. I had majored in Creative Writing and while the main reason I'd done that had been that it didn't require you to take any tests, I thought a career in writing sounded nice.

But I knew nobody was just handing out magazine jobs so I got busy, re-launching the then-defunct Trinity literary magazine, meeting with the HR people from Condé Nast magazines when they came to campus, getting an internship at *Hartford Monthly* magazine and begging the Trinity college paper for a job writing about…anything. (I ended up becoming the paper's restaurant critic.)

Still, by graduation time, I hadn't really figured much out. The Condé Nast HR department hadn't, in the end, been that wowed by my review of the Hartford TGI Fridays.

I've always been someone who is ready for things to end. I used to marvel at the other kids on the last day of camp as they sobbed and told each other they never wanted to leave. I enjoyed camp but still wanted to scream, "Hey guys, it's over! A month was the deal. And what are you crying about, anyway? We get to come back next year!"

College was different.

For the week after graduation, all our friends gathered at our friend Paul's family's summer house in Maine. For days, about 20 of us lived idyllically: eating delicious food Paul's mom made us, going on long walks and bike rides, drinking and sleeping and Jacuzzi-ing and pretending life would always be like this.

When Scott and I left Paul's and started driving toward Scott's family's place in Brooklyn, I started sobbing and didn't stop for days. We were going to spend a few days with his family and then I was going to move back home to Marin and try to figure out my next move.

I knew real life was beginning and the thought horrified me.

CHAPTER 5

The Baby Dragon

L OS ANGELES HAD ALWAYS beckoned me.
  I fantasized about LA the way other women fantasized about men. And actually my fantasies about LA were related to men because the men who moved to LA, I was sure, were my favorite kind. They were risk-takers. LA was a place where creative people flocked and lives could change overnight. It was sunny year-round.

The problem was, I didn't know how to get there.

My move back home after college had been brief—just a few months—and then I ended up in Manhattan, interning at a few different magazines and living with a roommate who moved out one Thanksgiving when I was away, saddling me with rent I couldn't afford.

So back home I went again, breaking up with Scott and, I thought, beginning an extremely glamorous life. Those glam fantasies were dashed, however, when I started the only actual magazine job I'd been able to procure—as an editorial assistant at *Parenting* magazine.

But I dove in, coming up with headlines for stories about Barney the dinosaur, writing articles about how nipples tended to crack during heavy bouts of breastfeeding and earning $17,000 a year.

During that time, I did my best to have fun in San Francisco. But the people around me only seemed to care about staying in the Bay Area and making money. Their lifestyle—traipsing around the Marina in fraternity or sorority sweatshirts after brunch, going out to see cover bands play at night—bored me.

I wasn't relating to my college friends either. They had all gotten so *serious*. People were adulting and I found it extremely disconcerting. They were talking about careers and finding life partners and I just wanted to keep having fun.

You could say their boxes had been packed and I was still wandering around, wondering if the box store was still open.

I knew Los Angeles was my answer. But how? I mean, obviously, I could have just moved there. But I wasn't, apparently, able to do that.

If I had a reason to move, I figured, then I could do it.

I imagined everyone wanted to live in LA and work for glamorous magazines, but some of us had to live in rainy cities writing about Barney the dinosaur until we had a reason to leave.

I would make half-hearted attempts to find a reason to move to LA or back to New York, reaching out to magazine editors in those places and sometimes even interviewing for jobs, but nothing ever came of those efforts.

And so I stayed at *Parenting* magazine in San Francisco for three long years.

Until I met Ross. My reason.

Ross was the brother of a girl I knew and when he and I met, drunk at a bar, we decided we would spend the rest of our lives together. Or actually, we took it a little more slowly than that: we met, made out, exchanged a few letters, met up again in Park City for the Sundance Film Festival and decided over the course of that drunken weekend that we were madly in love.

With all the confidence of a delusional, burgeoning alcoholic, I quit *Parenting*, packed all my worldly possessions into a U-Haul, moved with Ross into his Venice apartment and found myself, finally, in the city I'd always wanted to live in.

This went as well as could be expected, which is to say that within six months, we had one of those crying, screaming break ups that are always followed by one person coming to pick up their stuff when the other person is at work. In this case, I was the one who came home to find his stuff gone.

Despite the sunshine, I was broken hearted and friendless. Still, I'd managed to score my dream gig: as a writer for *People* magazine. And I'd managed to find people who drank like I did. I'd also managed to find a never-ending array of parties and events with open bars.

This all would have been fantastic had it not been so magnificently dysfunctional. And it was about to get a lot worse.

***

A year or so later, I sat at my coffee table, opening the contents of one of my dealer's packets onto my CD case before beginning my nightly ritual: chopping with the credit card, dividing, snorting.

Lighting a cigarette, leaning back, feeling that drip I had come to simultaneously love and hate beginning its descent down my throat, I stared at my phone.

I felt like I should call someone but wasn't sure who.

For the previous few months, I'd spent a lot of nights like this…by myself, doing cocaine, trying to rewrite a script. But then I would be stung by such intense pangs of loneliness that I would call people.

The problem was that I would spend the entire phone call wondering if whomever I was talking to knew I was high.

Staring at my phone again, I marveled at how quickly my life had gotten like this. Within two years of living in LA, I had lost my job at *People*, tried being an assistant at Disney and blown through a bunch of freelance jobs—the best being a gig writing script coverage and the worst being a dog walker for an Imagine executive who led me to believe that picking up her dog's shit was my path to a big-time career in the entertainment industry.

I'd also lost a lot of the friends I'd made and begun spending most of my time with fellow cokeheads. But those people had gotten annoying.

Spend enough time around fellow cokeheads and you can quickly see why: all they want to do is talk and most of what they have to say is nonsense. After a few months of regularly hanging out with these people, I'd found myself wanting to scream, "No, we're not geniuses coming up with ideas that are going to revolutionize the world! That's just the coke talking! And can't you just stop yammering for a second?"

One night I found my solution: just go home and do the cocaine alone. There was no competing for center stage because I was the only one in the auditorium. And there were no shitty business ideas that sounded great when there was cocaine sprinkled on them.

Instead, I decided I was writing the Great American

Screenplay.

That night, I decided I didn't need to talk to anyone. What I needed to do was write. I stared at my computer.

The drip dripped. I didn't move.

I lit another cigarette.

I needed more coke.

Then I got a great idea for a line in my script, the one that was going to move it from slush pile to bidding war. I took out the computer again and started writing it. But it wasn't good enough. I revised it. I lit another cigarette, then snorted another line.

I felt too high to write.

What felt like minutes later, I looked up from my computer and the birds were chirping. I could hear my neighbor Harry getting ready for work.

***

I heard someone once describe alcoholism as being like a baby dragon.

At first it's cute. A bit much, perhaps, but cute.

Then it grows older. It's not that cute. You kind of wish your friend who owned the baby dragon would leave it at home.

Then it becomes a full-blown dragon. Nobody wants it around. It doesn't fit in that one-bedroom apartment anymore. It's a beast, crumpling everyone in its vicinity. Beasts don't fit in the regular world but they don't fit in the "fun" world either because they take up too much room, leaving none for anyone else. And besides, the grown-up dragon feels ridiculous no matter where it is, all big and scaly and annoying. And so it stays by itself.

The problem is...the dragon is then all alone.

Add a whole bunch of cocaine, alcohol and cigarettes to the scenario and you have one very depressed dragon.

Another morning, much like the ones that had come before it, I was hunched in front of my computer, sure that the perfect line revision was just seconds away.

As I heard my neighbor Harry start his car, I took out my bottle of Ambien. I'd always had trouble sleeping and years earlier, I'd been prescribed a quarter of a pill a night. The problem was that a quarter of a pill was no match for two grams of cocaine so I had doubled, then tripled, then quadrupled my dose. And so on.

I didn't think of prescription drugs as drugs.

I thought I was doing what I needed to do in order to sleep.

Shaking five pills into my hand and washing them down with an Amstel Light, I wondered if these could kill me.

I welcomed the thought.

Because I knew that sitting there doing cocaine by myself, trying to write and never writing, was an awful plan.

I just didn't have any others.

And I needed cocaine. I knew I needed it because it was the only thing I had to look forward to.

I knew I couldn't live without it.

But I was starting to discover that I couldn't live with it either.

***

I have no idea what was different the morning I woke up in May, 2000 and decided to call my mom and tell her I was a cocaine addict. My family didn't know what was going on with me. They never asked a lot of questions about my life so I'd never had to provide many answers. I probably could have gotten away with what I was doing forever.

Still, I knew a call like this—"I'm an addict and I need help"—would get their attention.

I also knew about AA; I had been to meetings over the years. I knew they were horrible—filled with toothless men who chain smoked and talked about how they couldn't do the one thing they loved more than anything else.

I thought sobriety—recovery—sounded like just about the worst idea in the world.

There was only one thing that sounded worse: the way I was living. I was stuck between floors and I couldn't stand it anymore. Awareness without solution was killing me. They say that faith is belief despite lack of evidence. Somehow, that day, I had it.

The following week I was in rehab.

CHAPTER 6

The Dating Expert

"HOW ABOUT YOU COME on board as a columnist?" Michael suggested, smiling as he sat across the table from me at the Beverly Hills Hotel.

I swallowed, trying to make sense of what I was hearing.

Everyone knew that magazines couldn't afford to have staff writers anymore, let alone columnists. And yet there I was, sitting across the table from the newly appointed Editor-in-Chief of *Premiere* magazine and he was offering me this opportunity as casually as he had offered me a Diet Coke a few minutes earlier.

Premiere was my White Whale. When I'd lived in New York after college, I'd desperately wanted to be hired there and I'd actually interviewed for an internship position—a position that I later heard was snapped up by Regis Philbin's daughter.

Now, just a few years later, I was six months sober and being offered my dream job. *Regis Philbin's daughter who?*

"Um, yes!" I finally answered. I felt like my whole body was grinning.

Sobriety was like this. It was as if by going to outpatient

rehab and then AA, I had stepped into a dreamland where everything I'd ever dared to desire was being dropped at my feet. I'd spent the previous few years by myself, achingly lonely, mostly unemployed, high, convinced that recovery would be boring. It was anything but.

It turned out I'd had everything backwards. For one, I'd discovered that alcoholism really had nothing to do with drinking.

What I had learned in rehab and then AA, in short, was that alcoholics are born with a predisposition toward alcoholism that is either exacerbated or diminished based on what happens to them during their formative years.

The need to escape the pain of whatever trauma they experienced, combined with that genetic predisposition, cause them to use alcohol or drugs to numb. The numbing works amazingly well—until it doesn't. And the solution to breaking the cycle was, for me, astoundingly simple: working a 12-step program.

Discovering that allowed me to embrace rehab, AA and those steps like my life depended on it.

Then, within a few months of doing what was suggested—going to meetings, getting a sponsor, praying, taking inventory of my resentments and fears, embracing the fellowship—something shocking happened.

I didn't want to drink or do drugs. At all. I wasn't resisting. It wasn't willpower. My desire to do them had just evaporated.

It made no sense. I had spent the previous few years only thinking about drugs…when I would do them, how I would get them, how I would have to stop doing them. And then, after some incredibly simple actions that seemed wholly un-related to drinking and drugs, the obsession disappeared.

And there was this fact that the universe suddenly seemed intent on giving me everything I'd ever wanted. It's like the world had a whole bunch of presents lined up for me and was just sitting around waiting for me to wake up to receive them.

Most people's early recovery isn't like this. But mine was. I was about to go on a ride crazier than I could have ever imagined.

***

Antoine turned toward his assistant. "Hail that cab!" he said in his strong French accent.

The assistant, Louise, did as she was told and I quickly jumped into the cab, giving the cabbie a quick smile. I was wearing a yellow rain slicker—and nothing else. Louise threw a $20 bill in the cabbie's lap as I stepped into and then out of the cab. I did it again. And again. While Antoine photo-graphed me madly.

How had I found myself in this situation—naked except for a rain slicker, in Manhattan, being photographed by the man who had shot most of the Victoria's Secret catalogue?

Because life had thrown some crazy shit at me—good and bad—and I had surrendered to it all.

Six months into my job at *Premiere*, after I'd launched my column "Party Girl," interviewed a bunch of celebrities, gone to Sundance, the Oscars and the Golden Globes, the inevitable call came: cutbacks. I had been right in the first place—magazines really couldn't afford columnists anymore.

But, as a dedicated AA member, I accepted this news the way the people I'd heard in the rooms told me to: as a change

I should embrace. Rejection, I'd heard, was God's protection. Anything I wanted that I didn't get was happening because the universe had something far bigger in store for me.

Yet again, it seemed, those AA people were right. I accepted being let go from my dream job cheerfully and promptly got to work submitting articles to all my favorite magazines. Having been published in *Premiere* meant I was able to slide past gatekeepers at all the big magazines. Using the same energy I'd put toward recovery, I got articles published in *Cosmo, Redbook, Details, Vanity Fair, Self* and more.

And now, I'd made it to *Playboy*.

The stories for *Cosmo* and the rest of them had been either celebrity profiles or reported pieces, but *Playboy* had assigned me something entirely new: a first-person essay written by me and a New York-based writer about the experience of moving into one another's apartments and switching dating lives for a week. And they needed images to accompany that story. So they decided to make *us* the images.

In other words, I was three years sober and, against all odds, posing for *Playboy*.

To be clear: I was not naked. To continue to be clear: I was not *not* naked. Let's just say that pillows and shadows were used strategically.

***

Walking past security, I plopped myself into the makeup chair and Kristin went to work. Foundation. Blush. Lashes. The works.

And then it started.

"So…are you dating anybody?" she asked.

That familiar feeling of shame rushed through me. "No,"

I said. "I—"

"Shhhh," she stopped me. "Lips." Then she traced a bright red lipstick over my mouth. "Gorgeous!" she pronounced.

I could feel her about to start her questioning again when the segment producer Dan popped his head in. "How you doing, killer?" he asked me.

"Five minutes," Kristin responded for me as she gave my lips another coat. "I just need to finish her hair."

"She needs five," Dan said into his mouthpiece, giving me a thumbs-up and rushing back out of the room.

Miming for me to cover my face, Kristin took out a spray bottle as big as her arm. I put my hands over my eyes as she sprayed my hair, making it into one large shellacked solid piece. Then she plopped into a chair next to mine. "So what's his name?" she asked.

"Who?" I asked, buying time.

"Whoever you're dating!" she said. I knew if we had more than 30 seconds to spare she was going to whip out her phone and show me photos of her with her husband—a half Asian uncommonly built dude who gazed adoringly at Kristin in all their photos.

I also knew that she was just making small talk—she didn't really care about the answer—and that's what made the fact that I felt so ashamed about it feel even more shameful.

"I'm not…dating anyone," I finally responded.

She looked at me, shocked, even though it was the same thing I'd said the last 10 times she'd asked me. It was easier to tell her there was no one than to admit that I've gotten mixed up again with another guy who'd come on strong and then disappeared.

How could I tell her that the show's sex, dating and relationship expert—the woman who, after her *Playboy* story went viral, got hired on a TV show to dole out wisdom twice a week—was actually incredibly lonely?

I couldn't tell her that I was caught in a maddening cycle with Bill—a man who, after one date, had told me I was the woman for him and then, after a glorious few weeks, disappeared, only to reach out a week later to tell me the "situation had gotten way too intense" and he couldn't talk to me anymore.

I couldn't tell Kristin that this was actually my third cycle with Bill, who'd done the same thing to me two years earlier and then resurfaced after a year saying that losing me was the greatest mistake he'd ever made. Again, a glorious two weeks. And then he'd disappeared again.

Now here we were a year later. A month earlier, he'd reached out, telling me he understood why I'd never want to speak to him again. But, he said, he'd been in therapy and he now saw that I was the most amazing woman who'd ever lived and his one shot at happiness. Would I ever consider going to dinner with him, just once? That was all he asked.

Somehow, even though everything in me was screaming no, I'd said yes. We'd had a magical week-and-a-half. And then...silence. I'd reached out to him twice and hadn't heard back.

I couldn't tell Kristin or anyone else that every time Bill disappeared, it was like every bit of my childhood trauma descended upon me. I couldn't tell her that I had spent the last few weeks when I wasn't on set hysterical, unable to believe I was worth anything, wholly convinced I'd be alone forever. When Bill disappeared, I was transported right back to the car with my family laughing at me, right back to the top of the ski slope crying, right back to the card table where my grandfather was yelling at me that I was stupid.

I was all too familiar with the expression "Fool me once, shame on you, fool me twice, shame on me." And I was already all too familiar with shame.

I understood that what I was caught in had nothing to do with Bill. But the pattern he had me in—what scientists who experiment on rats call "variable interval reinforcement"—was as addictive to me as cocaine.

And it brought me just as low.

I couldn't tell anyone this because ever since the sensation of that *Playboy* story, I had somehow become the face of sex and relationships—the woman with all the answers.

It had all happened quickly. Turned out I had a real skill for faking it. Kristin was my makeup artist for a show called *Attack of the Show* that had hired me to do a twice-a-week segment with the show's co-host Olivia Munn.

It didn't occur to me to say that I couldn't do this job. I had continued to go with the flow that recovery had taught me: if this was happening, it had to be God's will. It's just that God's will, no matter how exciting, was starting to feel less good.

Dan popped his head in again. "Ready, killer?" he asked me.

"Ready," I responded, thrilled to be escaping from Kristin's line of questioning.

And then I went out onto the sound stage, where I answered people's sex, dating and relationship questions.

***

After a few years, the novelty of AA and recovery had worn off. Hanging out with my sober friends didn't seem to do it for me anymore. And while it was undeniably exciting to be on TV all the time, I felt like a fraud in my "dating expert" role.

I started to understand what people in AA meetings meant when they said that "cash and prizes" didn't bring happiness. I had been brought up to believe that success and money made you happy.

But the longer I was sober and the more "prizes" I accumulated, the more I started to feel the "hole in my soul" that I'd also heard people talk about in meetings.

After five years of being certain that sobriety and AA were the answer to everything that had ever ailed me, the elevator was once again completely stuck.

CHAPTER 7

If You Can Make It There

"YOU KNOW, YOU REALLY should just move here," Mark
said.

It was the day after my appearance on the show when the
host had asked if he could dedicate a segment to me. Mark
was a new friend—a gay guy I'd met because we'd both had
essays in the same anthology. And during this magical week,
which had included a lot of parties for *Party Girl*, he'd proven
to be a delight…planning karaoke nights and dinner, making
me laugh and just generally showing me how fun New York
could be.

I looked at him—and at midtown Manhattan behind him.
I took in the gorgeous summer day.

"But I couldn't," I said. "I mean, I tried living here after
college and it didn't work out."

"Sure. But how different was your life then?"

He was right. I had been young and silly and drunk. Now
I was an established writer. I already had my second book deal
with HarperCollins for a new novel. My agent was in New
York. My publisher was in New York. Who cared that I never
saw them? They were there. Writers belonged in New York.

"Very different," I responded. I could feel the sun on my arms, and myself warming up to the idea. There was a stirring inside of me; maybe New York was the answer to that tiny, consistent ache inside of me?

By the time I went back to LA a few days later, Mark and I had already started looking at apartments to share.

**

My favorite fantasy when I was little was "sitcom." Walking around my room re-arranging my Snoopies or petting the cat, I would pretend that a camera crew was shooting the opening credits for a show based on my life. Bouncy theme music would play as the sun shone through the windows on me.

That's how moving to New York in the fall of 2007 felt.

I would walk into a deli, order a salad and the man behind the counter would give it to me for free because I had "such a great smile." I would go into an AA meeting, share something and have a line of people waiting to talk to me after because they'd loved everything I'd said. I would go home to the apartment Mark and I had found on the Upper West Side and Mark and his friends would serve up delicious food on our patio and tell me how happy they were that I was there.

I had made enough on the new book deal and the movie rights for *Party Girl* that I didn't need to worry about money. And more money just kept flowing in—spokesperson jobs for Axe body spray, high-paying magazine assignments. Moving across the country hadn't even impacted my TV job. *Attack of the Show*, where I still doled out sex, dating and relationship advice, had agreed to fly me out to LA every month to shoot all the month's segments at once.

And there were men everywhere. Every week I had a date

with a different one and while I wasn't crazy about any of them, I definitely enjoyed the attention.

I soaked up the city. While I still had an apartment and car in LA and Mark and I were sharing a sublet, I could see that my next move was to go back to LA, pack up all my stuff and let the apartment and car go. How could I not? It was clear that New York was the answer I had been seeking! Why had it taken me so long to see it?

Sitcom music seemed to play behind me everywhere I went.

***

The difference between a New York winter and a New York fall is like the difference between prison and freedom.

One day, I was sitting with Mark in Central Park, brainstorming the new novel I wanted to write, feeling like I'd walked into a fantasy life, arranging to have all my belongings shipped from LA.

The next I was falling in the ice outside our new apartment.

It wasn't until we signed the lease that I learned the reason Mark was so eager to get a place with me: he and his former roommate had punched each other when drunk. As I watched him pour vodka over ice, I marveled at how thoughtlessly I made decisions.

But then I reminded myself: I had moved to LA without thinking it through and I loved LA. New York would be the same.

"I hope moving here wasn't a mistake," I said to Mark.

"Well, it's too late now." He downed his drink.

That was actually the last civil conversation Mark and I

had. Within a month, he was calling the landlord to say that I was inviting homeless alcoholics to move in when I let my sponsee crash on the couch and I was screeching at him that he was a drunk.

Within a month-and-a-half I had my own apartment in Chelsea. Another chance to start fresh. The only problem was that I was bringing me with me.

***

"How do you feel about writing under a pen name?" Paige asked me.

Taking a sip of my soda water with cranberry, I almost choked. "What?" I asked.

"You're such a great writer," she said, slicing into her steak. "And I'd really love to help you get away from the *Party Girl* sales records."

I swallowed. "It's that bad?"

She nodded briskly. "Not your fault. You know that." She popped a piece of steak in her mouth and slid a letter across the table.

I looked down at the letter. The restaurant was too dimly lit for me to actually read what it said. I could only make out the HarperCollins letterhead.

"They're mulching," she said, then went on to explain, "It's what a publisher does when they've printed more books than they can sell."

I stared at her blankly.

"They're destroying the copies of *Party Girl* that haven't sold."

I didn't know what to say. I'd written the book in six months without any idea, really, what I was doing. And it had been pure joy. I had no plan for it, no agent and I didn't care.

And then, the week I finished the book, two different agents emailed me. Both were fans of the column I was then writing for *Razor* magazine and both felt I had a book in me—and that I should reach out to them when I wrote one.

I responded to them both: I have a book in me! It's attached!

Paige was one of those agents. Within a week, she had sold my just-completed novel to my top-choice publisher, Judith Regan.

It was the ultimate publishing Cinderella story.

In the early 2000s, Judith Regan was it. She was the rainmaker. She made Howard Stern, Neil Strauss and dozens of others into bestselling authors. Every book she touched didn't just hit the bestseller list. It also created a sensation.

The year leading up to the release had been thrilling. My editor told me *Party Girl* was Regan's lead title of the season. They were trying to develop a reality show based on me to go along with the release. The buzz was so strong that magazines were reaching out to me about covering me and the book from the moment Regan acquired it.

And then, a few months before *Party Girl* was scheduled to come out, Regan released a book called *If I Did It* by OJ Simpson and all hell broke loose. Even though Judith's division, Regan Books, was reportedly responsible for half the revenue of HarperCollins, she was suddenly ousted and her entire imprint was dismantled.

Writers talk about being "orphaned" when their editors leave their publishing house for another. In my case, it was like being orphaned and then watching the orphanage burn to the ground. Most Regan book contracts were cancelled altogether and I kept being told that I was one of the lucky ones—my book was actually coming out.

But books need marketing and sales in order for readers to find them. While my book had gotten an insane amount of press and there had been a bidding war over the movie rights, a lot of buzz can only do so much. Without people to pitch it, *Party Girl* had barely made it to bookstores.

Sitting at dinner with Paige, I suddenly realized that we weren't just dining together because that's what agents do with their writers who live in New York.

No, she'd asked me here to let me know that it was midnight and it had turned out the slipper didn't actually fit me.

"Any word," she asked pointedly, "on the movie?"

I shook my head. I knew she already knew the answer.

The week of the book's release, the bidding war over the movie rights had culminated in a mother-daughter producing team outbidding everyone, including Melanie Griffith. They'd then hired the screenwriter who'd penned *Reality Bites*—the seminal movie of my 20s—to write the script. Over the previous few months, Paige and I had lunched with the mother and daughter several times to brainstorm casting ideas and make future plans. It had all seemed terribly exciting—lots of "Would Ethan Hawke be good for the love interest?" over lunches at Michael's on the Upper West Side.

A few weeks earlier, however, I'd received an email from CAA "congratulating" me on the fact that the movie rights had reverted to me. Confused, I reached out to the producing pair, but neither the mother nor the daughter returned my emails or calls. My film agent at CAA did eventually respond to me, saying, "Sorry it didn't work out. But you can still try to sell the rights on your own."

"Look, it could be so much worse," Paige said, bringing me back to the restaurant. "The Harper editors love you. They acquired *Bought*, right? Don't look so sad!"

I nodded slowly. *Bought* was my new novel; it was scheduled to come out in a few months and it sucked. I knew that. I wasn't sure Paige did.

Bought only existed because the day Paige and I had met with the Regan team about *Party Girl*, Paige had whispered to me as we walked in, "Hey, they may offer you a two-book deal. So have another novel idea ready."

Sitting down with Regan executives, I thought about a story Paige had told me that morning about another client of hers, a woman who worked for the government but was essentially a prostitute. At the time I had been working on a story for *Details* about hookers. And so, when Regan execs told me they were acquiring *Party Girl* and asked me if I had any other ideas, I told them that I wanted my second book to be a novel about women who were sort of but not quite hookers. They were just words coming out of my mouth, kind of like when I went on TV and gave dating advice I in no way followed myself.

"Ohhh that sounds good," a perky marketing girl named Samantha had said. "Yes, please. We want that!"

And so, in the year between Regan acquiring *Party Girl* and its release, I'd written it.

I hated every second of writing that book. I wasn't interested in hookers. But I was obsessed with the idea of being a successful author and I figured that with such a sexy topic, I couldn't lose. I had managed to make stories about Barney the dinosaur and cracked nipples from breastfeeding interesting. Surely, if I just tried hard enough, I could make a novel about hookers a sensation?

Paige liked the finished product. And so did Harper. They said they'd make an official offer once *Party Girl* was released.

And they had. The advance was half the size of the one I'd received for *Party Girl*. And I still hated the book.

But maybe, I told myself as I sat there with Paige in that dimly lit restaurant, I was just feeling burned. I had loved *Party Girl* with every ounce of my being and even though everything about its acquisition had led me to believe it would be a hit, what had happened since had proven to me that it wasn't.

Maybe, I thought, *Bought* was actually a really good book, too, and I was just protecting myself, the way a woman who's been spurned by a series of men won't allow herself to get close to any new ones.

Maybe this whole being-a-writer-in-New-York thing was going to work out just fine.

***

"We feel really terrible about what happened with *Party Girl*," Howard said. He squinted at me from across the conference table. "And we really wanted to make it up to you with *Bought*."

"We were definitely going to go wide with this," Samantha, the perky marketing girl who'd been in that first meeting where I'd pitched *Bought* enthused. "We really wanted to be able to build on all the press you got with *Party Girl*."

"Great." I nodded.

"Unfortunately…" Howard said, his voice dwindling off. He looked at Samantha.

"Bookstores really only look at how well your last book sold," she said. "And since bookstores really didn't have any copies of *Party Girl*…"

I nodded and looked around that windowless conference room.

"We still really believe in this book!" Howard said.

I didn't believe him for a second. Howard, I'd ascertained, was completely full of it. Over the previous year, after they'd acquired *Bought*, I'd re-read it and decided that it sounded completely inauthentic—that the fact that I didn't know anything about hookers was obvious in every sentence. I'd asked if I could have it back so I could rewrite the entire thing. Howard had said I could, but that I didn't need to. I'd rewritten it from page one anyway, and when I finished, I still hated it.

When I'd asked Howard what he thought of the rewrite, he said it was great. I was reasonably certain he'd never read either version.

***

What can I say about the three years that followed? The economy—and the publishing business—crashed.

Bought came and went quickly. I cared less about having another "disappointing sales" blunder on my record and more about the fact that I'd written a book I was embarrassed by.

And yet, when trying to come up with my next book idea, I didn't ask myself what I cared about or what I wanted to spend the next year of my life focusing on.

I had become obsessed with other people's success — writers I knew whose books had taken off—and I was convinced that it hadn't happened for me because I just hadn't hit the right topic. I kept thinking that if only I could find a topic the masses cared about, then I could finally have the success I should have had with *Party Girl*.

And then one day it hit me: the masses cared about reality television.

Reality TV had, of course, been a sensation for years. But I'd recently, accidentally, become a so-called expert on the topic. A few years earlier a producer at a new TV network called Fox's Reality Network had seen a freelance piece I'd written about *The Bachelor* and asked me to come on one of their shows to talk about it.

After my appearance that day, the producer had told me that the show needed regular "talking heads" —and also that it paid good money. Would I like to come on every week?

And that's how I'd found myself spouting off opinions every Friday for the next year alongside Kennedy, the former MTV VJ, about castmates on *Big Brother, Survivor, The Amazing Race* and others.

From there, an editor at the Fox News website had asked me if I wanted to write a column about reality TV. She could pay me a dollar a word.

It didn't occur to me to stop and ask myself if I truly wanted to write and talk about reality TV. Did I even enjoy reality TV? I didn't understand then that the opportunities we say no to are perhaps more important than the ones we embrace. I also didn't understand that I was operating from a depravation mentality. I subconsciously believed that every opportunity that came along was the last one.

Instead I thought, "This should be the topic for my new book! Everyone loves reality TV! And I have 'expertise' on the topic! If I do a book on it, how could it *not* be a hit?" I came up with the idea of asking the smartest writers I knew to write essays about their favorite reality shows. I would be attracting, I figured, the low brow (reality TV viewers) and the highbrow (fans of smarty pants writers).

Wasn't that everyone?

Wouldn't that guarantee success?

I pitched Howard and his team my idea: an anthology of essays on reality TV by 20 writers, curated and edited by me. Paige negotiated an advance that was half the size of the one I'd received for *Bought*.

I spent a year putting that book together, cajoling writers I knew and didn't know, until finally I had what I felt was a winner: an anthology of essays from writers Jerry Stahl, Neil Strauss, Neal Pollack and more.

And then. Zip, zilch, nada.

Yes, I did throw an amazing launch party—getting people from each of the reality shows we wrote about to appear alongside the writer who'd written about that show—and the media coverage was spectacular.

The media coverage was spectacular, however, because the *Bachelor* cast member who showed up admitted that the couple from the show had split. All the journalists who attended the book party only wrote about that.

It turned out reality TV fans wanted to watch reality TV and not read essays about it and fans of smarty pants writers didn't want to read what those smarty pants writers had to say about reality TV.

But I refused to give up.

***

"You just refuse to give up," Howard said. He popped a fried macaroni and cheese ball into his mouth. "I like that about you."

"Thanks," I said. I really hated the guy by then—the way he kept seeming so surprised by the fact that my books didn't "hit" even though he did nothing to help. But I was sitting at dinner with him and his boss Carrie to discuss a new book idea they had for me. So my hatred would have to be put on ice.

I didn't understand then that hating Howard was part of my problem. I somehow thought that subtle digs and barely concealed hostility would get him to finally be more support-ive, to act like he actually cared about me and my career. Only later could I see that my hostility surely only made him think I was a pain in the ass.

Carrie slid a pink book across the table for me. *Sex and the Single Girl* by Helen Gurley Brown. "It was the definitive guide on how to be a single girl in the 60s," she said. "All our moms read it."

I nodded. I'd heard of it. And of course I knew about Helen Gurley Brown, the longtime editor of *Cosmo*. Not only had I written for *Cosmo* but I also had friends who worked there and would tell stories about meeting with the legendary editor—how, even in her 80s, she wore leopard print from head to toe and purred, "Hey, pussycat" as a greeting.

"We were thinking you could do the modern day version of it," Howard said.

"Think about it: you could be today's Helen Gurley Brown," Carrie added.

I felt two things simultaneously—one was joy. They had not given up on me! After four books that had not earned out their advances, my publisher still believed in me. And they thought I could be the modern-day version of a publishing legend!

And then there was the other feeling. The one that said, "This is a great opportunity...for someone else." It was the voice I hadn't been able to hear when the *Attack of the Show* job had come up or when the opportunity to talk or write about reality TV surfaced.

At that point in my life, that second voice was still barely a whisper. I was too riddled with fear, too convinced that opportunities were going to be snatched away and too certain that everything that came my way was my last shot.

By then, *Attack of the Show* had replaced me with a mannequin named Uncle Ted, and shortly after that the show had been cancelled altogether. I was still going on TV doling out dating advice now and again but I was chronically single, dating a string of Bill types and feeling like a total fraud for giving anyone—let alone entire TV audiences—dating advice.

If I'd known then what I know now—that a career, and life, can be whatever we want it to be, if we have a strong enough vision of it—I would have stuffed another fried ball of macaroni and cheese in my mouth and told them that I just didn't want to write about dating anymore.

But I was in the elevator. I knew what I *didn't* want, but I couldn't see what the next floor looked like. And so I did what someone who's too scared to say no and too scared to say yes does. "I want to make this work," I finally said. "I just don't think I can tell single women how to live." I thought about it for a second and confessed, "I'm still trying to learn how to live myself."

By the end of the meal, we'd hatched a plot: the book would document me spending a year trying out everything that Brown recommended in *Sex and the Single Girl* and seeing how her advice played out in 2009.

"Year-in-the-life books are killing right now," Howard enthused.

He was right: *Eat Pray Love. Julie and Julia.* There was a book about someone trying everything Oprah recommended for a year, another one about someone saying yes to everything for a year, another about someone following all of Eleanor Roosevelt's quotes for a year.

By the time I hailed a cab to go home, I told myself to be excited: I was jumping on a trend! I had a new book deal!

***

All studies on happiness show that the most joyful people are the ones who have the most control over their circumstances. While I was ostensibly someone who had complete control over her life—I wrote when I wanted to, I didn't have a boss, I made my own schedule—I couldn't see that I was letting everyone else tell me what to do.

I may have called it allowing the universe to show me where to go, but really it was fear: if you tell me what to do, then I never have to ask myself what will make me happy. Plus, I can always blame you—whoever you are—if it doesn't work out.

I was still trying, desperately, to be popular. I had just

graduated to another level: instead of having Cory Carlson write nasty things about me in yearbooks, I had book critics, Amazon reviewers and Goodreads commenters to make me feel bad.

And if there's anything worse than feeling attacked and like every book you write is a failure, then it's feeling attacked and like a failure for agreeing to write books you don't even believe you should write.

I couldn't see that I was continuously putting myself in the line of fire without even asking myself what it was I wanted to risk being shot for. I didn't understand that embracing my own greatness—what made me *me*—was going to be the key to success.

I didn't understand that because I didn't know who I was. And I certainly didn't see any greatness there.

***

Of course I embraced writing the Helen Gurley Brown book, *Falling For Me*, in the same way I had the others. Like Howard said, I was determined.

Despite the fact that my dating life felt embarrassing and pathetic, I gamely went about trying all of Brown's recommendations—from wearing t-shirts with clever expressions on them to try to entice men to come talk to me to borrowing a friend's dog in an attempt to meet men at the dog park. While none of them "worked," I told myself they made for great material.

But I had really set myself up this time. The premise of the book, as conceived of by me, Howard and Carrie over fried macaroni and cheese balls that night, was that by the end of the year, I would become such an amazing version of myself that I'd meet the man of my dreams.

As the year ticked to a close, however, it still hadn't happened. I was dating a brilliant writer I could barely tolerate. His favorite activity seemed to be reading my work and pointing out the word repetition. My favorite activity seemed to be planning ways to break up with him.

By the time I'd finished writing the book, I had essentially given up on trying to make a career in traditional publishing work.

The elevator seemed perpetually stuck. I did all the things I had always done to be happy—going to AA meetings, working with a sponsor, going to therapy, meditating, writing. But the sitcom music was long gone. Still, I had convinced myself that I couldn't move back to LA unless I had something to show for this New York adventure.

I had to come back as a massively bestselling author with her own talk show. Or I needed to bring back a husband. At the very least, I had to be able to buy a house! But I was far away from having any of those things. I was stuck trying to figure out what writers were supposed to do when they realized their writing was no longer paying the rent.

A few years earlier, I'd been able to get a couple magazine stories a month and each would net me a few thousand dollars. Between that, book deals and *Attack of the Show*, I'd had no trouble paying rent on the overpriced closet I called home in Chelsea.

But in the months before the release of *Falling for Me*, I was in a panic. The economy had crashed—and taken the publishing industry with it. My days of getting $2 a word for magazine stories were long gone. I asked the girlfriend of my neighbor to coffee because she worked in advertising and I figured that might be an option.

She told me I'd probably have to start with an internship.

Then one day, a friend connected me with a guy she knew who was raising money to launch an entertainment website. They needed an editor. I lunged at the job—and got it. Or at least I'd have it, he promised, once they raised the money.

And then there were the snowstorms. Oh, the snowstorms. I'm pretty sure the winter of 2010 may have been the coldest, most stormy winter in the history of New York. Leaving my apartment meant putting on long underwear, two pairs of mittens, a hat, two pairs of socks, boots, a full-length wool coat and a North Face jacket that covered every inch of me...and I'd still be freezing. Sometimes the snow would be coming down so hard that I'd have to walk backwards to avoid being pelted in the face.

One day I was leaving the grocery store in that get-up and the overstuffed bag I was carrying fell apart on the street. As I watched my eggs crack and then freeze on the sidewalk, a man walked by and snapped, "Watch it" before shoving past me.

When I got home, I called my sponsor. "I don't think I can take it here anymore," I said.

"You don't have to," she responded.

And then I said what I'd been keeping to myself for the three years—something that had felt way too shameful to think, let alone say out loud. "I think," I told her, "I only moved here because I was convinced that I would never be successful or meet a man in LA."

"That's okay," she said gently.

"But it's not!" I shot back. "Think of all the money and

time I wasted!"

I will never forget what she said. "If all it cost you was three years and however many thousands of dollars to learn the lesson that you should never make a decision out of fear," she said, "I'd say you got the deal of a lifetime."

CHAPTER 8

La La Land

IN MANY WAYS, the move back to LA worked out gloriously. I was among people I'd known for years. It was sunny every day.

I even had, for the first time in a decade, an actual job with an actual paycheck; the entertainment website had not only managed to find funding but had also agreed to let me do the editing from Los Angeles.

And then, almost accidentally, I got a new book deal.

The first story I wrote for the entertainment site was an interview with a comedian who'd had a big career in the 90s and then lost it to addiction. Now that he was sober, he was getting his life and career back. And after meeting me that day, he wanted me to write a book about it. He paid me to write a book proposal and through an agent I knew, we were able to sell the book to Simon & Schuster.

If the sitcom cameras were following me, they would have shown the story I told myself I was living —as a website editor and celebrity book co-writer.

The truth is that there was no happy music humming in the background of my life then. It's hard to determine which of these jobs was more damaging.

The guy in charge of the entertainment site was the most brilliant, widely respected and emotionally abusive man I'd ever encountered. Other people at the site seemed to know how to let his barbs bounce off them, but I somehow couldn't. By reacting—getting defensive and accusatory—I always made whatever he'd done or said worse, which guaranteed that the cycle would continue.

But, I told myself, I wasn't relying solely on book deals to pay rent. I was getting a steady paycheck. There were no more snowstorms to wade through.

At least not literally.

But there was also the comedian.

***

"You and your fucking questions," the comedian growled.

He was sitting on the edge of his bed, hunched over, watching a video of himself singing with his band. At least you could call what he was doing in the video "singing" and you could call the people in the video with him a "band." In truth, it was a group of down-on-their-luck musicians who had agreed to play music while the comedian screeched into a microphone because they hoped his pseudo-fame would mean people might care.

"I've still got it," he mumbled. He looked up from the TV and at me. "Right?"

"Definitely," I responded. I was up against my deadline for the book and while my first few months of meeting with the comedian had gone okay, he was growing increasingly unhinged.

On a "good" day, the comedian was just inappropriate and not inappropriate and angry.

On a "good" day, the worst thing that happened was that he'd make me interview him in his bed. I told myself this was okay because it's not like he made me get naked or do anything with him. It was just the *concept* of a woman interviewing him in bed that he wanted.

And so I'd watch him crawl under the covers and I would get in on the other side and ask him questions.

On a "good" day, he acted like his answering my queries was a tremendous favor he was granting me —as if I were an eager beaver paparazzo who'd somehow broken into his apartment (and bed), rather than the person who'd sold a book about him to a Big Five publisher and gotten him hundreds of thousands of dollars as a result.

On a "good" day, the questions could be about his ascent —the big breaks, the potential he had, the famous people who'd sought him out. On a "good" day, I could leave his apartment, go home and write sections of the book.

The problem was that I was done with writing about the glory years and needed to get into the section of the story when everything fell apart.

This meant there were no more "good" days for us.

In the place of "good," there was a lot of swearing and avoidance. If he didn't like what I was asking him, he'd go into the bathroom and slam the door or call me names.

Watching the comedian gaze at himself singing, I decided I had the courage to get into the meat of the story—a massive scandal he'd endured and the reason Simon & Schuster had paid so much money for this book.

"Can we talk," I asked, swallowing hard, "about the trial?"

That's when the comedian flung the remote at his TV so

violently that I jumped.

"Fuck you, you dumb cunt!" he screamed. "You're even stupider than I thought! You just don't get it!"

I stood there. I nodded. I checked myself, emotionally, for bruises. I didn't seem to be crying. I was tough, I told myself proudly. This brute, pathetic man watching videos of his horrible singing and yelling at me for doing the job he had asked me to do couldn't hurt me.

***

"Let's work on getting you a job where no one talks to you that way, okay?" My therapist Lisa, who I'd been seeing since moving back to LA, looked at me from her chair.

I had just finished telling her about my day—an angry email from the website editor telling me that everyone hated me followed by the experience with the comedian. I told her how proud I was of myself for not crying about either.

"I barely even flinched," I added. "Isn't that amazing?"

I figured Lisa would think so. After all, she'd seen me the week before, the day the comedian had told me he'd only let me interview him if I flew his hooker girlfriend in from San Francisco. He'd tossed the pages of his book that I'd brought him to read in his building's incinerator. Then he'd thrown his phone at the wall behind me. When it had whizzed past my face, I'd started sobbing—and couldn't stop.

But now, I told Lisa, I'd become strong.

And that's when Lisa looked at me with that mixture of compassion and curiosity and explained that being able to weather abuse wasn't something to be proud of. "You shouldn't need to accept being spoken to like that," she said.

I looked at her, confused. "But that's just how it is," I

insisted. "To get what you want, you have to deal with horrible people."

She raised an eyebrow. "Do you?"

I thought about it. I'd worked for kind people, ones who didn't yell and throw things. But not in a long time.

She gestured around her office. "No one abuses me here."

I stared at her, realizing suddenly that many—perhaps most—women would have hung up on Bill the second time he reached out, quit the website job when they realized it was being run by an abusive man and not taken a gig writing a book for someone who was widely considered to be crazy and unstable.

While I'd always vaguely understood how trauma worked —that, in short, we spend a lifetime getting into situations that replicate what we went through out of a delusional belief that we'll finally get it "right"—Lisa was the therapist who got me to see how much I was hurting myself through this process.

I didn't quit the website job or working with the comedian, but in a way, the elevator was finally moving again.

***

I kept seeing Lisa for years.

In that time, the book for the comedian had been released and become a *New York Times* bestseller and both the abusive website editor and I had been fired from the site.

I had also launched my own website and sold it for six figures within a few months. I told myself I was a badass entrepreneur. I created something with a few hundred dollars and was able to spin it into literal gold!

I told myself this so I could avoid the reality: the person I had sold the site to was crazier than the website editor and comedian put together. I'd known him for years and his rage and insanity was so pervasive that I'd avoided him at all costs.

But still I chose to sell my business to him.

In many ways, it was easier to deal with the site owner than the editor and comedian—primarily because I could go weeks without hearing from him. He didn't ever make me get in bed with him or tell me everyone hated me.

In other ways, he was worse than the others, primarily because he told me my job depended on me lying for him. When the company lawyer, who happened to be his best friend, asked me point blank one day about something my boss had told me to lie about, I told the lawyer the truth.

A minute later, I got a call from my boss. "What the fuck were you thinking?" he asked. "It's like my wife asking me if I wanted to fuck you!" he raged. "Of course I do! But you don't tell her that if she asks you!"

Then there was the day he changed the name and content of the site without telling me. When I went to the home page and saw that the website I'd created had a new name and different content, I called him.

"You should be grateful!" he shrieked. "I'm saving your ass! No one wanted to read what you were writing."

I'd been hearing I was ungrateful from my dad my whole life. And what was I going to do? This guy controlled my paychecks. And so I corralled my team and explained that we were now a site about something entirely new.

There would be months of relative peace followed by sudden calls from the owner that I had to fire someone or cut $20,000 from the budget that day. I would do as I was told.

I told myself I was lucky. I was making okay money. I was

relatively unsupervised. And I had a great team who worked for me.

Because of my great team, I also had downtime during the day. And that's when I started trying to think of another plan.

***

It was becoming increasingly clear that I couldn't stay working at the website. Not only was it being run by a lunatic but also, clearly, the lunatic's plan hadn't worked. He had told me when he acquired the site that we were going to be making hundreds of thousands of dollars in ad revenue. Three years later, after more budget changes than I could count, it was clear that was never going to happen.

And so, when a woman reached out to me and told me that a niche magazine she'd started had been acquired by a manufacturing company and they needed an Editor-in-Chief, I thought it was my way out.

For one, it was a print magazine.

Secondly, it was owned by a manufacturing company. Surely, I thought, they had to be legit?

By then, the website owner had informed me that he could no longer afford my salary. He hadn't fired me but he hadn't *not* fired me. And so I flew to the Midwest to meet the manufacturing people.

***

"The truth is, Ben controls everything," David said as we walked back to the office.

I had just finished lunch with David and two of his colleagues—overweight men in suits who didn't say much. At lunch, I'd been able to ascertain a few key facts: one, that David and the two overweight men had worked together for years—before the manufacturing company they'd been at another company that a man named Ben had started.

Oh, and two: Ben was in prison.

It was all starting to make sense.

Earlier that morning, David had introduced me to his boss Pat, explaining that Pat was Ben's son. Pat, who appeared to be in his late 20s, spent our meeting alternating between playing video games on his computer and reciting goofy facts. While David and the two fat men didn't scream "wildly competent," they did seem able to form clear sentences.

"So Ben put Pat in charge but Pat really doesn't do anything?" I asked quietly.

David nodded. "You didn't hear it from me," he said softly.

"What, exactly, is Ben in prison for?"

That's when David said a whole bunch of words that didn't make a lot of sense. I might as well have been put in a time machine and sent back to the conversation with my dad when I was 16 and he was talking about his embezzlement. Lots of "it's just what any smart businessman would do" statements combined with phrases like "making a scapegoat" and "didn't do anything wrong."

"When is he getting out?"

"In a few months," David said. "By that time, you'll have already made the magazine a success."

I smiled. "So that means I got the job?"

"If you'll take it."

After working for a series of name-callers and phone throwers, you'd think "prison boss" might have set off an alarm bell. But it didn't. The truth is, I looked at David—sweaty, with a paunch and a nervous smile—and thought, "I can control this man. I can win."

Standing in the unseasonable mugginess, I suddenly remembered something I hadn't thought about in a long time—how, when I first moved to LA and wanted to be a screenwriter, I would always meet male literary agents who would ask me out. I'd think I could use their interest in me to get them to sign me as a client. It never worked. We would go out on a date, I would attempt to turn their romantic interest into a professional one and they would agree to read my script. Then when I wouldn't want to kiss them, they'd feel rebuffed and I'd never hear from them again.

Standing there with David, I suddenly realized that I had delusionally believed I could outsmart the casting couch—that I could make men *think* I was going to sleep with them just long enough for me to get what I wanted.

It never worked. And yet I kept thinking it would.

Then a word floated through my mind: faith. Ever since getting sober, the concept had been drilled into my head that whatever was happening was God's will. And that meant everything was unfolding as it was supposed to. I'd assumed that all that had happened in my career—from the *Playboy* story to *Attack of the Show* to the book deals with Harper to Bill and the other men to the editor and the comedian and the website owner—was meant to be.

It hadn't crossed my mind that maybe God's will was for me to see these options and say no to them so that I could see what might happen if I had a little more faith.

Standing there in the sunshine, this thought flitted across my mind. The problem is I didn't listen to it.

CHAPTER 9

The Prisoner and the Plagiarist

"BEN DOESN'T WANT HER on the cover," David told me when I was a few weeks into the job and we were getting ready to close the November issue. He was talking about the celebrity we'd been able to cajole into appearing on the cover of our craft magazine. "He wants it to be a dog."

"I'm sorry? A dog?" I stared at the phone.

"Um, yeah. And well…" David was the kind of person who didn't think hard very often; when he did, you could hear it over the phone. "Are you comfortable communicating with Ben directly?"

Communicating with a prisoner was something I hadn't done before, if you didn't count the handwritten letters I'd received at my PO box from prisoners who'd seen me in *Playboy* or on TV. But the fact that Ben wanted to replace our celebrity cover subject with an animal—indeed, that he wanted an animal to be the "face" of a craft magazine— needed to be dealt with hands-on. I figured if I explained a bit about how magazines worked—namely that the cover image had to correspond with the magazine's theme—he'd relent.

"Great." David sounded relieved. "I just have to get you

signed up as someone the prison allows to contact him."

And thus began my communiqué with Ben—and Perry.

No one ever clarified to me who Perry was—Ben's prison mate? Lover? Old pal who just happened to be in the clink with him? All I knew was that these two prisoners, both of whom appeared to be barely clinging to literacy, were suddenly emailing me at all hours, telling me how to run the magazine and what to put in it.

Because Ben was aware of the fact that it was illegal to run a business out of a prison, he always couched his orders as "suggestions." He called himself an "advisor" and Perry a "fellow advisor."

Over the phone, David made it clear that I had to do everything they said.

At first, it seemed almost sweet—these two clueless old men pretending to be magazine publishers from their cells. But rather quickly I realized that they may have been clueless and they may have been old, but there was nothing sweet about them.

I originally tried communicating with Ben like he was a child. "It doesn't make sense to have a dog on the cover of the magazine," I had written to Ben on the day David first connected us. "Because it's a craft magazine and because celebrities sell copies, the best thing we could do would be to have a celebrity who does crafts."

I added that we had already done an interview and photo shoot with the celebrity and that when a magazine made that arrangement with a publicist, you had to stick with it.

Ben was having none of it. He wanted a dog—his reason being that he firmly believed they were man's best friend.

I kept trying to explain that it did not make sense to have a dog on the cover.

I got nowhere.

By then, Perry had discovered his inner Shakespeare and penned a book called *101 Ways to Thrive*. He emailed me one day to tell me that he believed it could change the world. He added that he and Ben had decided that they would like to honor me with the opportunity to write the book's foreword.

At first I said yes. This was my job. Yes these were some wackjob crooks but hey, I figured, this is the price you pay to be the Editor-in-Chief of a print magazine.

The next day, when Ben threw down the gauntlet—he was "advising" me that there would be no more discussion and the dog would be on the cover so I had to figure out how to explain the situation to the celebrity—I thought about what I'd agreed to.

By then, Perry had sent me the "book" he'd written, which he'd referred to in the email as an "insta classic." It was, unsurprisingly, thoroughly incomprehensible. And here I was, a *New York Times* bestselling author who'd agreed to attach her name to it. Out of what? Fear? Obligation?

Perhaps buoyed by the thought of his upcoming literary fame and fortune, Perry had by then become an idea machine: his new flash of brilliance was that he wanted me to create an infomercial about his book using my "celebrity friends." It would be very easy, he insisted. After all, I lived in Hollywood so I could surely find a studio that would let me shoot there for free. And I could definitely figure out a way to make a video that would go viral. He was sure of it.

And that's when I realized just how much I'd been putting

up with. Without thinking too much about it, I wrote Perry back. "I can't do that," I wrote. "I have the magazine to edit." I added that I'd thought about it and didn't feel comfortable writing the foreword for his book.

For three days, I didn't hear from the prison men, David or anyone from the manufacturing company. This was odd; since I'd taken the job the month before, they'd all been reaching out to me at all hours. It was even more odd considering the magazine had to be closed and shipped soon.

I could sense something was amiss. I just didn't know what.

***

"I am shocked and horrified," David's email began. He went on to tell me that he and his team had spent days going through the content for the November issue—all content they had approved weeks earlier—and discovered that the stories in it had already appeared in other publications.

A bit unclear on the concept of freelance writing, he then added that he was horrified to discover that the writers I'd assigned stories to also wrote for other publications.

His conclusion? I was a plagiarist who hired plagiarists. He would, he explained, have to hire a "forensic detective" to comb through the stories I'd put together for the November issue to see which were "legitimate."

I had used all the same writers who'd written for me for years at different websites, none of whom were plagiarists or who wrote the same stories for multiple publications.

But I understood. David was like a scared little boy typing words he didn't really understand. I figured he didn't know that it's actually a big deal to accuse a writer of being a plagiarist, that he'd picked up the term "forensic detective" from a cop show he'd watched while shoving Red Vines in his mouth one night and that he had been Ben's whipping boy for so long that he didn't actually understand what he was saying... just that he needed to do *something* to get rid of the woman who'd dared to say no to his boss's prison pal.

The email ended with the pronouncement that I was being fired, effective immediately.

Call me a wimp but hearing you're a horrible plagiarist even if you aren't and being told you're so immoral that detectives need to be hired to look at your work, even if that's the most asinine sentence you've ever read, hurts.

I let myself cry. But I never let myself be sorry for saying no to Perry. Because, even then, I could see that saying no hadn't been the problem. The problem was that I'd been saying yes for way too long.

***

For some reason, after the craft magazine and website jobs wandered into the ether, I wasn't scared. I should have been. But I wasn't. The elevator was somehow moving, even if I had no idea where it was going.

The day after I received David's email, one of Ben's other lackeys reached out to me asking me to sign a mutual non-disparagement contract.

I wrote him back and said that they were welcome to disparage me all they wanted to—they could announce to all that I was a plagiarist who hired plagiarists and that they needed to bring in forensic detectives to read the work.

Unless, I added, they wanted to pay me.

I thought I might get somewhere with this. These were

criminals, I figured. And criminals could have both a lot of money and a lot to hide.

But I got nowhere with this lackey. He kept trying to explain in new ways and with different words that they could *really* damage my reputation if I didn't sign their paperwork and that it would be in my personal and professional interests to do exactly what he said.

I kept trying to explain to him in new ways and with different words that they could say whatever they wanted about me and in turn I would say whatever I wanted about them.

Unless they paid me.

This exchange went on for some time until the day I realized that if I took their money, I would be just like them. While sure, I'd never commit whatever fraud Ben and Perry had committed to land in prison, free money from these guys wasn't ever going to be free. I wrote the lackey back saying they could forget about paying me, but I still wasn't going to sign anything.

I never heard from any of them again.

***

While I was figuring out my next move, I experimented with saying yes to writing other people's books.

Basically, ever since my book for the comedian had come out and become a *New York Times* bestseller, other people had been asking me to write their books.

But the phone throwing and bed interviewing and name calling had taken everything out of me. While I knew that no other future subject could possibly be as awful to work with as the comedian had been, the experience had soured me on writing books for other people.

Still, I had time while I was figuring out my next move so I agreed to do two different book proposals —one for a former Miss USA who wanted to become a recovery advocate and one for a woman who went by the moniker of The Queen of Versailles. Both of them believed that their stories would incite a bidding war—or at least a bite from a small publisher. Neither proposal sold.

Through those experiences, I started to see something that I'd been slow to realize, something the universe had been trying to tell me since my last book: traditional publishing was over. While I'd been able to get $50,000 for *Party Girl* back in the early 2000s, that just wasn't happening anymore. The only new people publishers were giving book deals to were those with massive social media followings and email lists.

Traditional publishing didn't care how good a story was. It may have never cared. But now the odds of success were getting slimmer.

My friends from the traditional publishing world—the friends who had sold big books to major publishers—were either contemplating going back to school, working at celebrity weeklies or embarking on entirely new careers. I realized then that traditional publishing was a rigged system—destined to only work for the Elizabeth Gilberts, Glennon Doyles and whoever else happened to have a book really hit. As my friend Jennifer Armstrong told me when I had her on my podcast, "There are levels internally that publishers don't tell you about, and when my book hit the first week, it felt like I had unlocked this whole new level in a video game that I didn't know existed. On my previous book they'd all been very polite, and said things like, 'Here is another thing someone has written about you. I am passing it on,' and that was kind of it. Now they were saying, 'Do you want to have a marketing meeting?' I'd say, 'I thought we already had that meeting.' And they essentially said, 'Sure, but do you want to have a *real* meeting?'"

I saw, way later than most, that the majority of the writers who pass the Rubicon by getting a deal were going to end up disappointed and broke.

Then I looked at self-publishing: an entrepreneur and author named James Altucher who'd done several books with big publishers, wrote a book called *Choose Yourself*. He hired independent editors, cover designers and everything else.

It sold 45,000 copies in the first week.

Other names were popping up. Amanda Hocking. Mark Dawson. Nick Stephenson. People were doing the thing I'd long derided—self-publishing—and making not just a killing but also an impact.

I'd had everything backwards. Or the world had changed. It was time for me to change, too.

***

"I think we should work together," the email read.

It was from a sober guy who told me he was really passionate about making an impact in the recovery world. Usually the people who sent me messages like this were eager but a little Perry-like, minus the cell: they all thought along the lines of "let's make a PSA about my book that goes viral!" They didn't understand that it took more than being passionate and having a random idea to make an impact.

But this guy was different; for one, he was a sports agent who represented Magic Johnson, Hulk Hogan and Dennis

Rodman. And secondly, he was willing to fly out from New Jersey any time I'd be willing to meet with him.

And so I sat down with Darren Prince the next week. I couldn't figure out if he was for real. He cried when he talked about visiting one of AA's co-founders' homes but also seemed to run in the fastest of fast circles.

We brainstormed possible joint ventures: an online summit or an in-person event. He seemed game for whatever I wanted to do. Then he said, "Why don't you write my book?"

I was just coming off the experience of writing book proposals for the former Miss USA and current Queen of Versailles. Both Miss USA and the Queen had blamed me for the fact that publishers didn't want their books. Both of them found other writers after me and neither proposal ever sold. This had made me renew my vow not to write anyone else's story.

But Darren seemed wholly unlike them—not delusional at all. Still, I wasn't willing to risk it. "I just don't think I have it in me to write another person's book," I said. "I'm so sorry."

"Think about it" was all he said.

When he called the next day, I said I couldn't do it.

Darren was insistent. He called me every day for the next few weeks and taught me that there was a way to be persistent without being annoying. Finally, a thought occurred to me.

My friend Kristen had recently reached out asking if I could help her get work. She was an amazing writer, an *LA Times* bestselling author of multiple books and, like all the other talented writers I knew, struggling to make ends meet.

The next time Darren called, I pitched him on the idea of my friend writing the book. "Could that work?" I asked.

"As long as you edit it. I want your stamp on it."

And that's how it happened. I negotiated a deal with Darren and with Kristen and edited the book Kristen wrote for Darren.

When it was done, Darren announced that he wanted me to publish it.

I laughed. "I'm not a publisher!" I said.

"That's okay. I'll pay you to figure out how to become one."

And that's how I became a publisher.

Darren arranged for parties in New York, Miami and LA. He got himself booked on every TV show known to man. The next thing I knew, he was on Jordan Harbinger's podcast, then Lewis Howes'. The week his book came out, he landed a six-figure spokesperson deal with a rehab. He was suddenly getting huge speaking gigs. He even created the Aiming High non-profit.

I had accidentally become not only a publisher, but a publisher with a hit book.

***

But then something even more significant happened: I became friends with Joe Polish.

One day I was on Facebook and saw a video interview my friend Tommy Rosen had done about recovery with this affable guy named Joe. Joe had a way of speaking about addiction that I hadn't come across in my years of sobriety: he was honest, pragmatic and compassionate. He talked about leading high-ticket events and feeling so empty afterwards that he would hire hookers. He talked about wanting to change the global conversation about addiction from one of judgment to one of compassion.

When I Googled him, I was even more surprised. Apparently, he was considered the "world's best connector." He hung out on Necker Island with Richard Branson. He was friends with Tony Robbins and Arianna Huffington. And he was talking about sex addiction in interviews?

On Facebook, I saw that my sister-in-law knew him. I asked if she would connect us.

And that's how I found myself a month later in a Beverly Hills hotel room being interviewed by Joe for a documentary he was making about addiction. I didn't know it then, but that meeting would change the entire trajectory of my career.

"Come to dinner," Joe texted me later that day. I had met him earlier, interviewed him for my podcast, been interviewed by him for his documentary, gone to breakfast with him and one of the biggest marketing experts in the world and had just driven back to Hollywood.

"When and where?" I asked.

At dinner in Beverly Hills that night, I sat at a table with Joe, his team and some of the world's most successful entrepreneurs. Sitting across the table from Dave Asprey, the creator of the Bulletproof phenomenon, I could barely cut my chicken.

Yes, I'd been in Hollywood since the 90s and in that time rubbed shoulders (and more) with plenty of celebrities. Sure, I'd dated Matt Damon in college. But the allure of people who were famous for standing in front of cameras saying other people's words had worn off.

People who created businesses that had influenced thousands if not millions of people, on the other hand? People who were so kind and helpful and welcoming that they treated me like I'd been sitting among them for years? People who fought over who'd pick up a check for 25 people?

My whole life, I'd been seeking rules for living. The ones I'd grown up with—get a 1600 on your SATs, go to Harvard, make money at whatever cost—hadn't worked for me. When I found recovery at the age of 30 and was introduced to the 12 steps—when I learned rules for living that had to do with being of service, getting rid of resentments and developing a spiritual connection—I knew I'd found a better philosophy for me.

But I'd never had role models. I'd always believed that I had to make a choice—I could either value money or I could be an artist.

Sitting at dinner, it occurred to me that perhaps there was a way to do both. I felt a bit like the sort of person you hear about who becomes a lawyer and then, during a midlife crisis—perhaps post Porsche but pre-mistress—realizes that all his life he wanted to be a writer but he'd just been subscribing to the values he'd grown up with and not realized he could listen to his heart.

I was the opposite. In my zeal to be as different from my family as possible, I'd assumed I'd have to always scramble and take scraps from phone-throwing comedians and law-breaking Midwesterners. Sitting with Joe and his friends, I saw there was nothing wrong with making money. It allowed you, after all, to graciously pick up a dinner bill for a bunch of people you didn't even know. It gave you the luxury of being able to think big rather than small. I saw that I had been in such a blind panic to make money my whole life that I'd never had the time to stop and ask myself what my unique abilities were and how I could use them in ways that were the most beneficial to me and others.

It was just going to take one final kick in the ass for me to see I was worthy of joining the table.

CHAPTER 10

Launching Into a New Life

MY MAJOR TRANSITION STARTED, of course, with a break-up.

I had been in a serious relationship with a man for nine months when, quite cavalierly, he informed me that he wasn't interested in being in a relationship anymore.

It wasn't me, he explained. In fact, he was still quite willing to keep having sex with me. He was just done with the caring-about-me part.

I was devastated.

It's not because this man was so wonderful. He was a skinny, bald, nerdy struggling filmmaker who liked to call himself an "artist." He was also the worst version of someone who likes to call himself an artist because he was always convinced that his big break was coming any second.

But he made me laugh. And what can I say? My standards still weren't very high.

Most of my friends never understood why I even liked him in the first place. So when I fell apart after the break-up, they were mostly flummoxed. I heard a lot of "He was a loser" and "You know you can do so much better" and "Why do you care so much?"

At the time, I wasn't sure why I *did* care so much.

The best sense I can make of my devastation after this break-up is that I'd constructed an elaborate fantasy of this extremely ordinary man I was dating and one day, he revealed who he really was and the shift between my fantasy and the reality was so sudden and extreme that a lot of my childhood trauma surfaced.

Suddenly I was sobbing all the time—so hard that, one day, walking down the street, a homeless man stopped to ask me if I was okay and when I defensively told him that I was, he observed that I didn't look okay.

When homeless people are asking you if you're okay, it's time for a radical act. For me, that radical act was EMDR.

EMDR, for those not fluent in therapy speak, stands for Eye Movement Desensitization and Reprocessing and it's the most effective treatment that exists for trauma. It is, by most people's standards, a bad name for an amazing tool—bad not only because it's a hard-to-remember mouthful but also because you don't need the eye movement component for it to have a lot of effect. Nowadays, most EMDR practitioners have the client either wear earphones that play alternating beeps or hold orbs that alternate pulses between the right and left hand.

In the same way that a woman nearing the age of 40 knows her first mammogram is looming, I always knew I was headed for EMDR. I had just hoped to put the experience off for as long as possible.

Over the years, friends of mine who had also experienced trauma had tried it out and they always reported that it was "amazing" and that they'd sobbed during and after. While the words "amazing" and "sobbing" don't go together in my world unless you're talking about *Terms of Endearment* or *Beaches*, I was still game. I knew, because I had occasionally hysterical reactions to situations that were not hysteria-inducing, that EMDR was probably the cure. Most of us don't wake up one day and say, "What do I feel like doing today? Oh, maybe I'll make an appointment for something that will make me sob uncontrollably!"

But I figured since I was already sobbing uncontrollably all the time, why not go to EMDR? At the very least, it would give me a new place to cry.

Now, I'm as woo-woo as can be. (I was once so close to my tarot card reader that she texted me from the hospital to tell me her granddaughter was born.) But even I have a hard time believing that EMDR works as well as it does. Still, studies don't lie and an abundance of research shows that EMDR is better than any other treatment that exists for PTSD.

And I can't deny what happened. I sat down, cried my eyes out about the break-up, my new therapist Anadel handed me some pulsating orbs and we got to work. Rather quickly, we connected this guy's behavior to similar things my family had done—and eventually to my core belief that unless I was adored by someone I'd assigned power to, I was worthless. We were then also able to piece together that because the love I'd been given growing up had been so arbitrary and sporadic, I only felt comfortable in situations in which people had one foot out the door. I had come to equate unavailability with love. And I had undervalued myself for so long that I didn't know what it felt like to have supportive, loving people in my life.

This was something I had understood to varying degrees before EMDR, but the realization had always ended with, "So what?" I would talk about my patterns and talk about my patterns and end up… repeating my patterns.

But Anadel and I dug in there.

The science behind what's happening in EMDR is this: the bilateral stimulation that the pulsating orbs provide, in conjunction with revisiting a specific memory, causes the neurons of our brain to re-wire so that we have a different relationship with that memory. Even more significantly, we are able to experience a different reaction to whatever we encounter that triggers a subconscious memory of that trauma.

Within a few weeks of twice-weekly sessions, I had an astounding revelation. I had accomplished quite a bit in my life and was an altogether fabulous person with many gifts to offer the world. I cannot emphasize enough that these were things I had not seen, even when people complimented me about them.

That's because the only people whose words I allowed to mean anything were the people in my family. Ever since I'd started to find success, I'd send them my books and articles and tell them when I was going to be on TV. They never read or watched any of it and it would kill me.

Through EMDR, I discovered that I continued to see myself the way they seemed to see me—as someone flailing around, trying hard, but ultimately doing nothing. The strangers and acquaintances who complimented me had to be mistaken or giving me far more credit than I deserved. *She is confused*, I would tell myself. *His opinion doesn't count*, I'd decide for some reason or another. In short, nearly every nice thing anyone had said about me, since the beginning of my life, had not registered because I had not allowed it to.

EMDR untangled all these tendrils to make me see that my family would never acknowledge me and that it had nothing to do with me. I remembered when I introduced my mom to Matt Damon and she said, "He thinks he's going to be an actor? He's not even cute." A few years later, he was on the cover of *People*'s Sexiest Man Alive issue. I could become president, cure cancer and set the world record for saving the most orphans and they would never, ever acknowledge it. I had to stop seeking their approval.

While that may never happen—I don't know if I'll ever reach a day when their indifference will no longer hurt— EMDR showed me that I had, quite literally, never seen myself as the truly spectacular creature that I am. Suddenly, I saw myself. And I really liked what I saw.

I realized something else, too. For as long as I could remember, I'd been trying to succeed in situations that were rigged against success—whether it was making a living through traditional publishing, working for abusive people or dating men who behaved like children.

It will be different for me, I would tell myself. *I'm powerful enough to make that person change*, I would think. I didn't see that there's nothing admirable about surviving a game with no winners. I'd had the good sense as a kid to opt out of dodge-ball. I could opt out of these games, too.

Until EMDR, I didn't see that true victory wasn't surviving a game in which people are throwing metaphorical balls at you from all sides. It was finding a new playing field. It was inventing a new game.

***

After Darren's book came out, the clients just started popping up. A South African businessman heard me on Joe's I Love Marketing podcast and reached out to see if I could have his book written and published. Another Canadian rehab owner asked Joe who he should have help him and he hired me, too. By then Joe and I had partnered on a number of projects—cowriting *The Miracle Morning for Addiction Recovery* with Hal Elrod and helping to develop his Genius Recovery foundation.

In one year, my publishing "side hustle" netted me more money than I had made in all six of my book deals combined. But far more than the financial rewards were the personal ones: I was helping people share their stories.

Most of them were entrepreneurs—people who had built up massive businesses because of their expertise. They weren't writers, but they had wisdom and stories to share, and sharing that wisdom and those stories was taking their businesses to new levels.

I quickly built up a stable of other writers, most of whom had worked for me at other publications. I found cover designers, layout designers, developmental editors, copy editors and project managers. I was able, in essence, to take what I'd learned from going through the churn of traditional publishing and give clients everything I felt I hadn't gotten myself.

Building up this company hasn't been easy. Some clients are so challenging that I regret ever taking them on. But their demands and complaints teach me more than my easier clients, mostly because they remind me of what it took me so long to learn: next time I know in my gut I'm talking to someone who will never be pleased, I get to opt out of working with that person.

Despite how challenging someone is, I remind myself that no matter what they say and do, whether they're thrilled or upset, I am here to help them share their stories. I am here to facilitate the process of helping them take a mess—which is to say, a life—and make it into a message.

But here's something else I've realized: we can't make our mess into a message until we know what our mess really is. For me, it took 20 years of therapy, 17 years of 12-step work and 15 years of meditation to even get to the point of being able to approach the form of therapy—EMDR—that helped me finally see how I'd let the way my family treated me dominate my self-perception.

It took going to EMDR, week after week, reprocessing the worst memories, for me to see that I'd been accepting the unacceptable for years. It took seeing and feeling that for me to be able to fall for a man who wasn't completely self-absorbed and destined to disappoint me. And it's taken over a year of being with him for me to fully surrender to what it's like to be adored and supported and loved.

My elevator ride from little girl who never felt seen or heard or acknowledged to woman who tries to help others feel seen and heard and acknowledged has been my journey—my mess. And that's what makes it my message.

Whatever your version of a mess is, it can be your message. And then it can be your memoir.

PART 2
THE MESSAGE

CHAPTER 11

Making *Your* Mess Into *Your* Memoir

I F YOU'VE MADE IT THIS far in this book, my guess is that you're more than ready to take your own experience and make it into a memoir that can help other people.

There are just a few things for you to figure out first.

First and foremost…

Determine Your Message

Determining your message is, as far as I'm concerned, the only crucial thing you need to know before you start writing. Otherwise, you risk doing what I did—flailing around with multiple books that ultimately mean nothing to you.

If you're not certain what your message is, I highly recommend working with a professional writer. Of course, hiring a great writer (and there's no point in hiring one if you're not going to hire a great one) isn't possible for everyone.

So if you want to get started on your own, ask yourself: what is my story? You have one. We all do. And if you can tell it well, you can change the world. People often come to me concerned that their story isn't compelling enough. I always confess that my story isn't that compelling and yet I've made it into seven (eight, counting the one you're reading right now) books. It is not about how interesting the story is. It's about how it's told.

In conceiving of your message, here's how I recommend looking at it: What is the most valuable lesson you've learned? This will change over time. For me, 15 years ago, recovery took center stage. After going through my career and personal experiences and then landing in EMDR, I realized that my message was about seeing, feeling and sharing how my struggles had shaped me so that others could do the same.

Determine Your Why

Writing a book, whether you're doing it on your own or with help, is a massive undertaking. It might take a good deal of time or money to get through to the other side. The best way to set yourself up for the moments when your commitment may waver is to get extremely clear on *why* you're sharing your story.

My why, when I wrote *Party Girl*, was what I told you at the beginning of this book: I thought if I could make the tiniest bit of a dent in the perception the world had about addiction and recovery, I could maybe help people from having to go as low as I had gone.

I didn't expect it to lead to TV show appearances, TEDx talks or any of the other gifts it brought. But those gifts taught me another solid why.

Over the years, I've watched dozens of our clients reap incredible rewards from their books. Darren, in addition to all the other gifts he's received, has told me repeatedly that the book gave him his life's purpose.

Another client, Emily Lynn Paulson, took the memoir she did with us and landed on *The Doctors*, got a TEDx talk and grew a recovery coaching business.

Then there's Matt George, the CEO of the Children's Home Association of Illinois, who went from behind-the-scenes guy to center stage after his book came out. He's now giving keynotes in front of thousands of people, doing podcast interviews every week and watching his social media following grow 10-fold.

Those are just a few examples of hundreds that I could give. I've watched clients add $500,000 a year to their bottom line and land more of their own clients in a year than they had in all the previous years combined, simply because the people they were doing business with knew their personal stories and thus trusted them in ways they hadn't before.

But I can also give you examples of people who put all the same effort, time and money into a book only to have a nice object on their shelves. The difference between those people and ones like Darren and Emily and Matt is that the latter had a very clear idea about what a book could do for them.

They knew their why. And they followed it. Because of that, they changed lives—most notably their own. Still, you don't have to want to be front and center. There are all sorts of reasons for wanting to write a book that don't include appearing on TV or growing your business.

Maybe you just want personal freedom or to help people. In this Instagrammable world, where there are so many people out there perpetuating the story that having everything we want is easy, we can all do our part to tell the gritty truth.

Whatever your goal is, let's move on to *how* to write your book.

Learn The 10-Chapter Format

While you can follow any chapter format you'd like, I recommend using the 10-chapter format below (also broken down in the Memoir Download I told you about in the beginning). Here it is:

Chapter 1: Intro/Inciting incident/Flashback/Turning point

Chapter 2: Childhood/Adolescence

Chapter 3: The path (whatever it is…career/personal story)

Chapter 4: Escalation

Chapter 5: More escalation

Chapter 6: Hurdles or problems

Chapter 7: Turning point

Chapter 8: Path toward resolution

Chapter 9: Resolution

Chapter 10: Life after resolution

Let's break down each of these.

The rationale behind making the first chapter a flashback is that it brings us smack dab into the apex of your story. You're more likely to get us engaged if you deliver us a heightened moment.

You do this because you want an audience immediately engaged—you want the reader thinking, "This person has a crazy life, I want to know more." That way, they'll be more invested in the second chapter—your childhood and adolescence.

Then, in the third chapter, you're getting on the path. The word "path" depends entirely on the story you're telling. Is it a tale of overcoming abuse or addiction? Is it about swimming with the sharks as you climbed the corporate ladder? Whatever your path is, chapter three is where you lay it out.

In chapters four and five, the action escalates. If it's a memoir about building a business with a morally corrupt partner who ended up fleecing you, this is the part when you're thrilled as you watch the money roll in and marvel at both the skills of your chosen partner and your luck in having aligned yourself with him. Escalation is when everything is exciting; in chapter four, the wheels haven't yet fallen off the bus.

That all changes in chapter five. In recovery, people use the expression "First it was fun, then it was fun with problems, then it was problems." Chapter four is still fun; chapter five, less so.

And then, in chapter six, the fun screeches to a halt. This is when incidents that, in retrospect, couldn't have lasted come to a grinding halt. The tax bill arrives. You miss a crucial event because you're drunk. The buck has stopped.

In chapter seven, something shifts: there's a hint of a different way of living. It's when, to stay with the scenario of the crooked business partner, you see that there actually might be a way to start a new business without him. In the recovery memoir scenario, you meet someone who's sober and successful and happy. Chapter seven is when you haven't arrived at a transition point quite yet, but there's a glimmer of hope that it's possible.

And then there's chapter eight, in which you prove the shift *is* possible because you take one tiny step toward it. You tell your wife that she's been right this whole time: the business partner has to go. You start calling rehabs.

This sets you up for the real transition in chapter nine: the resolution. You officially make that business partner a *former* business partner. You check into rehab. Chapter nine takes us through you finding out what life is like without whatever it was that you never thought you'd let go of.

And that brings us to chapter 10: life after resolution. Today, or something close to today. This is the chapter that focuses less on tentpole scenes and more on the comparatively peaceful day-to-day existence you've achieved as a result of this journey.

And there you have it. Your (former) mess. Your message.

Select the Right Scenes

If the 10-chapter structure I just detailed sounds overly simplistic, know one thing: it is.

But simple is not the same as easy.

One of the most challenging tasks, once you've determined your message and your why and are ready to get started, is going to be determining which scenes you're going to use.

I recommend selecting between three and seven scenes for each chapter and really fleshing them out. A laundry list of what happened is going to read like, well, a laundry list. Instead look at your life and ask yourself: what are the incidents that really shaped me?

This can be inarguably challenging. You may be thinking, "You're asking me to pick three events from my entire childhood? Are you kidding me?"

I get it. There's a reason "kill your darlings" is a common quote about writing. But having too much to pick from, as opposed to not enough, is a quality problem.

I recommend asking yourself: What are those memories that are stuck in my craw or that I've discussed repeatedly in therapy? Still, it's important to make sure you balance out the more damaging incidents with happier times. There are very few times in our life where only terrible things happen (except, perhaps, in chapter six).

In this book, I realized I had to skip huge chunks of my life in order to tell the story. I distilled the three years after college into five paragraphs, simply because, in retrospect, nothing that happened felt crucial or helped move my story along.

You get to do the same. There's no detective who's been by your side your whole life and is going to rail against you for not sharing about times in your life that aren't relevant to the story you're telling.

You get to decide what matters. Isn't that fun?

Understand That It's About You But It's Not About You

As you take us through your story, the most important factor to keep in mind is that it is for us. Your readers.

I spent so much of my career thinking, "I should write about this topic because it will be a hit" or "I should write about this topic because the opportunity is here so it must be fate." I didn't think: what have I experienced that can help people?

Choosing to write about something because you think it will hit still makes it about the writer—what the writer thinks. But what does the reader think? What does the reader want?

It may help to picture one person—your ideal reader—and then multiply that person by a thousand.

They say the riches are in the niches because it's true. And it's never too early to start thinking about your niche.

I often think about what Ryan Holiday wrote in *The Perennial Bestseller*: that his first book, *Trust Me, I'm Lying*, was geared toward people who worked in social media.

Not people who *use* social media. People who *work in* the social media business.

A slim segment of the population, no?

That was his point. If you conquer a niche fully, that niche will become your fan base—the beginning of what Kevin Kelly calls your 1000 true fans.

I also think about an anecdote I heard when I first started studying marketing. It was about a lawyer who created a course called "How to Get Clients." No one bought it. So he changed the course to "How Lawyers Can Get Clients." A few more people bought it. Then he changed it to "How Lawyers Can Use LinkedIn to Get Clients." It sold like crazy.

So how do you find your audience? You can simply go look for books like yours. Start by checking out books you know of, then do simple keyword searches on Amazon. And pro tip: if you want to know what you can include that your competitors have not, check out the one-star reviews and see what readers complain is missing.

Once you figure out who your audience is, you're going to have a much easier time sharing your message with them.

KEY TAKEAWAYS: The 5-Step Process for Making Your Mess Your Memoir

1) Determine Your Message. Ask yourself: What is the most valuable lesson I have to share?

2) Determine Your Why. Ask yourself: Do I want to just help people, build a business, launch a speaking career, get more clients, all of the above or something else?

3) Follow The 10-Chapter Format:
Chapter 1: Intro/Inciting incident/Flashback/Turning point
Chapter 2: Childhood/Adolescence
Chapter 3: The path (whatever it is…career/personal story)
Chapter 4: Escalation
Chapter 5: More escalation
Chapter 6: Hurdles or problems
Chapter 7: Turning point
Chapter 8: Path toward resolution
Chapter 9: Resolution
Chapter 10: Life after resolution

4) Select the Right Scenes. For each chapter/time period, ask yourself: What are the 3-7 incidents that really shaped me?

5) Understand That It's About You But It's Not About You. Ask yourself: Who are my ideal readers? How can I find them?

CHAPTER 12

Once You've Finished Writing

NOW THAT YOU KNOW how to write a book, let's talk about how you can publish it. The first step is to educate yourself.

Educate Yourself About Traditional Publishing

If you're determined to pursue traditional publishing, here's how it works for non-fiction: you'll need to find an agent who will submit your 25- 60-page book proposal to book publishers. (Yes, you could submit yourself but I don't recommend it—not only because agents understand contract nuances we don't but also because most reputable publishers won't work directly with authors.)

Know this going in: even after you're signed by an agent, it's really, really, really hard to get a publishing deal today; the rough statistic is that two out of every 10,000 book proposals submitted to major publishing houses sell. It also takes a really, really, really long time for a book to see the light of day— usually a year or two between when a publisher acquires your book and when it's released.

If a publishing company does acquire your book, however, there's good news: they cover the costs of editing, designing and releasing. In exchange, they own the rights and make all decisions about the cover, title, release date and everything else (with your input, of course). Once they earn back your advance, you then theoretically start earning royalties (the rates vary but it's usually been between eight and 25% of the book sales), This is theoretical, however, because only about 25% of books ever earn out their advances.

The rewards of traditional publishing are undeniable—especially if you're published by one of the Big Five publishers. Your book is legitimized in the eyes of many and your chances of hitting bestseller lists and getting covered by the media are better.

The misconceptions people have about traditional publishing are also undeniable. Everyone I know who tells me they want to be published traditionally gives the same reasons —they want to hit the *New York Times* bestseller list, they want to be sent on a book tour, they want the support a big publisher provides and they want their books in stores.

Here's what I can say to that: the chance of a book hitting the *Times* list is miniscule and putting your focus on that is a great way to make your book release experience miserable. (I know because I did it—five times!) The one time I *didn't* obsess over a book of mine hitting the list, it *did* hit the list. And while it's undeniably cool to be able to dine out on being a *New York Times* bestselling author (and trust me, I have), focusing on that as a goal is, I think, to miss all the potential joys of the publishing experience.

In terms of a book tour, I personally know almost no one

who has been sent on one—and I know a hell of a lot of traditionally published authors. I guarantee Elizabeth Gilbert, Glennon Doyle and all the authors who don't need book tours are sent on pretty plush ones, but the authors I know who "go" on tour are often paying for and arranging those tours themselves.

As for publisher support—look at it like this. Imagine you're a filmmaker and you get a studio to invest in your movie. Yahoo, you've made it! And this isn't just any old movie but one you wrote and are directing, producing and starring in. And you're not just starring in it—you're the *only* star. The year that you're shooting, the studio is very supportive. Lots of patting you on the back and giving you advice. Then it's release day. You're a bit scared by the fact that, er, nothing seems to be happening. So you reach out to the studio...and don't hear back. You're confused. Weren't you all in this together? Didn't they give you money so you could all have a hit on your hands?

So surprising is this experience that every time it happened to me, I basically suffered something close to amnesia and therefore had to go through it six times in total before I finally got the memo: my publisher wasn't going to do anything for me. The reality is that publishers pick a book or two a season to put all their efforts behind—and my books never made the cut. All the major media exposure I got for my books I secured myself. That's because the chosen ones are the ones that don't need support. Howard's indifference to my books wasn't per-sonal; he was just going for low-hanging fruit.

As for having your book sold in bookstores, HarperCollins paid for each of my books to be in stores for a few weeks. Then the books slowly, with each purchase, dwindled out of the store—never to return. The reality is that most books that aren't instant bestsellers don't stay in stores—unless the author jumps in. (More on that in a minute.)

I don't mean to sound discouraging. I just mean to sound realistic. And there's a reason that, after six traditionally published books, I wouldn't go traditional again.

So let's move on to the other options.

Educate Yourself About Self and Hybrid Publishing

Self-publishing isn't what it used to be back when your great aunt paid a janky publisher to put out your family history and foisted the copies upon every family member over the holidays.

Instead, these days, it's possible to publish a book yourself that is indistinguishable from a book published by, say, HarperCollins. If you're going to achieve that goal, however, it means that you must strive for excellence at every stage.

The time frame is—well, it's whatever you want it to be. While I highly recommend taking your time with it, Amazon allows you to replace a book with an updated version at any time so it's possible to launch a book, re-do it and launch it again. Still, I don't recommend that. "You only get one chance to make a first impression" is a cliché for a reason.

Then there's what we do at Launch Pad—which is called hybrid or indie publishing. In this case, a client hires us to write and publish or just publish the book. The client pays for the entire process, keeps all the proceeds and rights, and makes all final decisions about content, cover, release date and everything else.

Of course, deciding which way you want to go in terms of

publishing isn't the end of it. If a traditional publisher acquires your book, they'll be taking care of a lot of what follows in this chapter. If you're publishing yourself, this will fall on you.

So what's next?

Come Up With Your Title

Who doesn't love coming up with a title? Answer: so many that often people have theirs before they even start writing their book.

Many also change their titles along the way—and for good reason. Tim Ferriss's first smash hit, *The 4-Hour Work Week,* was originally called *Drug Dealing for Fun and Profit.* I can't tell you why it had that title but I can give you a 100% guarantee that it wouldn't have sold over a million copies if he had kept it.

When I first wrote *Party Girl,* I was enamored-verging-on-obsessed with the title. At the time that my agent signed me, however, she told me she couldn't submit a book called *Party Girl* to publishers because a book with the same name had just come out. So we sold the book to Harper under the title *The After Party.* In the year between acquisition and release, that other *Party Girl* book sold so poorly that we were able to revert to my original title. (Fun fact: that other *Party Girl* was written by Rachel Hollis, the mega bestselling author of *Girl, Wash Your Face.* It's safe to say everything worked out okay for her.)

When coming up with titles, always aim for clear over clever. It may be tempting to want to include a reference to something in the book but if readers don't get it, they're unlikely to want it. When *Bought* came out, it seemed like a pretty straightforward title. Well, I can't tell you the number of people I spoke to about the book who would respond in a way that made it clear they thought it was a tech book called Bot. (If you ever find me writing a tech book, by the way, please have me arrested for fraud.)

Another fact to keep in mind is that most non-fiction books have subtitles. Here's why: a title is meant to attract attention and a subtitle is there to clarify what the book is about. A subtitle also, in this Amazonian world we live in, gives the author a chance to use keywords (more about that in a bit). The fact is, Amazon is the third largest search engine in the world (right after Google and YouTube) and some readers are going to find your book by typing something into the search bar. A subtitle with keywords that people are searching for frequently will come up.

Still, don't obsess too much over keywords. When you think about why you read a book, chances are it's because a friend or someone you follow wrote or recommended it. So while some readers are going to find your book by searching, most are going to read it because it's worth recommending.

If you're worried a subtitle will weigh your book down, consider this: one of the most popular books of the past few years is Mark Manson's *The Subtle Art of Not Giving a F****. What most people who recommend it don't even think about is that it also has a subtitle. But do people say, "Hey have you read *The Subtle Art of Not Giving a F***: A Counterintuitive Approach to Living a Good Life?*" No, they just use the title. Same with another incredibly popular book of late—Jen Sincero's *You Are a Badass*. Its subtitle is *How to Stop Doubting Your Greatness and Start Living an Awesome Life*. Did you know that? If yes, please email me and I will personally buy you a copy of that book because your attention to detail and memory are beyond impressive.

(You may notice this book doesn't have a subtitle. That's for two reasons—one, as I mentioned, I'm experimenting a bit here and two, my title is clear enough that I felt like a subtitle would be redundant. Like a bad parent, let me just say "Do as I say, not as I do.")

Once you have your title, you move onto the next —and frankly most laborious—stage. Don't say I didn't warn you.

Rewrite

If you're going with a hybrid publisher, the publisher will take care of the rewriting process. At Launch Pad, we do a first draft and then a rewrite based on the client's feedback.

If you're rewriting on your own, one option is to start every writing session by re-reading what you wrote the day before. But know that this can be a rabbit hole so if you believe you may get lost in an endless rewriting loop, I recommend that you start rewriting only after you've completed your draft.

Whenever you rewrite, just know you're doing it to streamline and look for repetition. But it's also possible to err on the side of not reinforcing who, say, a character is enough. Keeping the reader informed but not overly informed is a delicate art. The rewrite is the time to refine it.

You're also looking, on this first rewrite, to simply make sure your book makes sense. Is the content in the right order? Do all the scenes work? Is the wording correct and the flow working?

While I don't have a specific routine for rewriting, my

friend Paul Shirley does. He suggests giving the first draft to one person and asking that person to let you know five things they like and three things that need work. After rewriting based on that feedback, he recommends giving that draft to five different people who have different perspectives—say, Mom, college roommate, work partner, casual acquaintance and cousin. You're basically looking for as disparate feedback as you can. He recommends then taking months away from your book before rewriting again.

Your own rewriting process is going to depend on you. But I will offer one last piece of advice: be careful who you trust with your manuscript. We're all fragile flowers, especially when it comes to our creative work. Find supportive people but urge them to be honest. "I loved it" isn't, after all, feedback we can use.

Once you've rewritten (and possibly rewritten again), you move to the next stage: getting professional help.

Hire an Editor

There are several different types of editors and rounds of editing and it's crucial that you understand who does what and when.

The first round is the developmental edit. This is the edit that's a lot like what you did when you were rewriting—but it's done by an unbiased professional. He or she is looking for inconsistencies, less-than-smooth flow and to possibly move sections around. This editor isn't focused on tiny grammatical corrections but rather on major changes.

Next the manuscript goes to a copy editor who will focus on tiny grammatical corrections. This person is looking for missing words, incorrect punctuation and consistency on editorial decisions, such as whether or not to use Oxford commas, whether or not to write out numbers, whether or not to italicize book titles and websites…factors that may seem insignificant but are obsessed over by people like me.

A proofreader generally follows a copy editor because even though a copy editor is trained to look for all those niggly, tiny corrections, that copy editor is a human being and will thus make mistakes. The proofreader is there to catch them.

Even with all those editors, however, there will probably still be mistakes. It's frustrating, but so many books have been published with typos that you can find countless stories online that show different typos in major literary works. The good news in self and hybrid publishing is that, as I noted, you can correct and replace a manuscript easily.

In order to decrease your chances of publishing a book with typos, you might consider recording your audio book at this point. (More on audio books in a bit.) There's no better way to catch errors and other small bits you want to change than by reading your work aloud. If you're not ready to commit to an audio book, you can also try using programs that will read your work out loud to you.

When hiring an editor, err on the side of caution. I can't count the number of clients who have come to us at Launch Pad with books that they say are edited —and that need a complete overhaul. That's because anyone can call him or herself an editor and what the word "editor" means varies a lot. Your book could need a developmental edit (and if you're new to writing, it probably will) while the person you hire is only equipped to fix typos.

To avoid running into trouble with this, have a clear conversation with every editor you consider hiring. Get on the same page about what they plan to do. If that person hasn't worked on traditionally published best-selling books, ask for references. In some cases, potential editors will be willing to edit a sample chapter.

Because Launch Pad editing is limited to Launch Pad clients and we run on the pricey side, I keep a running list of freelance editors and cover designers who are available for hire. I don't know these people and therefore can't vouch for their services but I do know that they work as editors. You can find the list at www.launchpadpub.com/editors-designers-more.

Once a book is edited, you may have one more step before getting the book laid out.

Consider Any Potential Legal Issues

If you're writing about real-life experiences in a book, I highly recommend including a disclaimer; you can even go ahead and copy and paste the one I use in this book. I also recommend changing the names of the people in your book, unless they tell you not to or it would stand out as just plain odd (like, say, changing the name of the spouse you're going to thank profusely in the Acknowledgments).

Even with names changed, there can still be legal issues and if there's anyone you're writing about who you feel might object to how they're portrayed, err on the side of caution.

When I went through *Party Girl* with a lawyer, she gave me a rule of thumb that I recommend following: if you're including a character based on someone who could object to their portrayal, try to make sure that person is described in a way that makes it not entirely clear who it is. In other words, do not describe a character based on someone you know who has one leg, lives in Ames, Iowa and works in cryptocurrency. The more vague and less unique the details are, the better. You can always alter details to make someone less identifiable.

While we recommend that any of our clients who have any concerns at all hire a lawyer to review their books before publication, not all do. As a result, we've had instances in which objections came up immediately before publication; lawyers had to be brought in at the 11th hour and changes had to be made. I don't want that to happen to you.

We also had a client tell her company that she was doing a book but didn't show them the content. Her supervisors objected to some of the material in it and she almost lost her job as a result. So if you're not a free agent—by which I mean if you're associated with any sort of corporation, society or group that might object to anything in your book—have the manuscript approved ahead of time.

Once it's approved, you get to move onto another fun stage: thanking the people who have helped get you to this point.

Write Your Dedication and Acknowledgments

So who do you want to dedicate your book to? You don't have to dedicate it to anyone but if you want to, it can be either a person or a group of people. Some of the dedications our authors have used, just so you can see the variety, are:

To la mia famiglia

To all social service team members all over the world who
are heroes to many

To Evan

Then there's the Acknowledgments section, which you
can think of as a Dedication times 10 or 100, depending on
how many people you include. It appears at the end of your
book and it's where you thank everyone who's helped you
with the book *or* everyone who's helped you on your journey
to get to this point in your life. (My Acknowledgments section
for *Party Girl* was so long that I even thanked a certain
Trader's Joe snack I ate obsessively while writing it; *Los Angeles*
magazine warmly mocked me for it.) Most books include an
Acknowledgments section.

Hot and/or manipulative tip, depending on your point of
view: If there's a well-known person you don't know but
who's been an inspiration, you can include that person in your
acknowledgments. This gives you a lovely excuse to reach out
and send that person a copy of your book when it's out.
Maybe you'll garner a new, high-profile fan.

Next up: an opportunity for validation.

Gather Blurbs—and Possibly a Foreword

Some books have forewords and a foreword is exactly what
it sounds like—the words before the words. It's written by a
luminary that has a close relationship with the author. But
don't stress about it because this section isn't at all necessary.
Have you ever bought a book because of who wrote the foreword? (Here's another opportunity to get a free book; email

me if you have and I'll send you another copy of that book because you are one dedicated fan of that foreword writer.)

A foreword can absolutely provide legitimacy so if there's someone you know who's either incredibly well-known or extremely well-respected in your field, you can ask that person. If it's someone who's quite busy (which, of course, can go right along with being incredibly well-known and well-respected), you can offer to transcribe their thoughts into a foreword they approve.

If there's someone you feel you can ask for a favor but not quite as big a favor as a foreword, why not ask for a blurb? Blurbs, also called endorsements, are those quotes from well-known people about how amazing your book is. In a pinch, you can always use a quote from the foreword as a blurb. You can also, in a pinch, use a quote that's about you and not about the book.

While blurbs are also not required, most books have them. At Launch Pad, every book has at least one so that we can put it on the back cover but we've had authors who've gathered literally hundreds. Just like with a foreword, it's unlikely that someone will buy your book because of the blurb, but they do provide great "social proof" that you can use everywhere—on your book, in your book, on your website and on Amazon. You can also make blurbs into share-able cards for social media.

One factor to keep in mind: asking someone to blurb your book is a massive favor. I'm someone who is both asked to blurb and also asks others to blurb books so I speak from experience when I say that you shouldn't ever expect someone you don't know to do it.

The best way to have success with a blurb request is to make it entirely clear why you're asking this person and then show just how grateful you are to them to even consider doing it.

When I first started publishing books, I simply didn't understand what a big favor I was asking. I was so excited about my book that I delusionally believed whoever I was asking should be, too. It was only when I started blurbing other people's books—and being on the receiving end of some of the most presumptuous requests and kindest thank you gestures imaginable—that I realized how unappreciative and presumptuous I'd been.

Give your blurber time to read your book—ideally at least a month—although if you're requesting a blurb from someone who you theorize may not have time to read the entire book but would like to support you, you can offer to write the blurb yourself and just get his or her approval.

Now that you've gotten some validation for just how awesome your book is, there's a necessary but simple technicality to handle.

Come Up With Your Price

There are all sorts of opinions out there on pricing, so I'll just tell you what we do at Launch Pad: we usually price our paperback books at $12.95 or $15.95 and our ebooks at $9.95, although if an author wants another price, we go with that. If your book is on the shorter side, you should price it for less. Keep in mind that you can always change your ebook price later.

If your book is available exclusively on Amazon, you can also make it free upon release or down the road, and have it listed on freebie newsletters to drive it back to the #1 spot.

This is a service we provide for clients but you can easily do it yourself; just Google "KDP free book" for information on how.

You can also give your book away for free using a site called BookFunnel. BookFunnel accounts cost $100 a year and allow you to create landing pages for multiple books where anyone can download a PDF or an ebook in exchange for their email address. If you're sending out regular emails (more on that in a bit), you know how valuable that email address is.

Now onto another simple but crucial task.

Get an ISBN

Contrary to popular belief, you don't need to copyright your book since books have an automatic copyright as soon as they're published. The only reason to have your book copyrighted is if you end up getting into a legal battle with someone because you believe they've plagiarized your book; in that case, you'll have far more power if you have a copyright.

You do, however, need an ISBN—an International Standard Book Number—and you need a different one for each version of your book (paperback, ebook and hardcover if you're doing one). You can purchase ISBNs from a company called Bowker. The cost diminishes greatly if you buy in bulk (it's $125 for one, $575 for 100) so if you think you're going to be publishing more books, why not buy a bunch?

While Amazon provides free ISBNs for anyone who published exclusively on Amazon, I recommend splurging on your own since you may want to have your book available on Nook, Apple Books and elsewhere.

Once you have your ISBN, you can easily convert it into

a bar code for your paperback. Download the bar code and give that to your cover designer to place it on your back cover.

Did I mention cover? Yes, I did. That's because we are, at last, at this stage.

Have Your Cover Designed and Your Book Laid Out

I've told you not to skimp on an editor. It's also important to put some money toward a cover. While you can use a free cover from a site like Canva.com or even create one on Amazon, the cliché that you can't judge a book by its cover is an outrageous lie.

A cover could be the difference between someone buying your book and skipping over it entirely. As I mentioned in the Editors section earlier, you can access a list of cover designers for hire at launchpadpub.com/editors-designers-more, but as with the editors on the list, they aren't people I've worked with before so do your own due diligence.

While I also have layout designers listed on that page, you can use your own layout software for your actual manuscript —Vellum is considered the best of the bunch but for now, it's only available for Apple.

If you're doing a hardcover as well as a paperback, you'll need two different covers; almost every cover designer will happily do the additional one for a nominal fee.

Which brings us to…

Decide If You're Going to do a Hardcover

Most authors these days create ebooks and paperbacks but skip hardcovers. Here's why: hardcover books can cost the author up to $13 apiece, take months to print and aren't purchased as often as paperbacks and ebooks.

Like it or not, the majority of your readers will probably be buying your book on Amazon and for the moment, Amazon only prints paperbacks. Still, the fact that they offer print-on-demand at all is pretty spectacular.

Here's why: authors used to have to provide Amazon with books. Now, whenever someone orders your book, Amazon custom prints and ships it without charging you and instead subtracts the cost from your earnings. You keep 60% of standard distribution and 40% of extended distribution to bookstores and libraries.

Still set on hardcover and want it on Amazon? No worries. You can list it for a nominal fee in the IngramSpark catalogue, since they have a distribution deal with Amazon. If you're not going to be buying bulk copies to hand out or sell yourself, you won't pay more than the Ingram fee.

But that's not the only decision to make about ways readers can get your book.

Decide If You're Going to do an Audio Book

Oh, audio books! Where would we be without them? Answer: a lot less well-read. The rough statistic is that 50% of American adults have listened to one and my guess is that 100% of authors have.

Once upon a time, Audible had to buy your audio rights for your book to become available as an audio book and they only purchased a tiny percentage of the books out there. If they bought your book, they paid for studio time, production and a narrator (or for you to record the book yourself). Then, in 2011, Audible created ACX, which allows any author the opportunity to record, produce and upload a book and have it sold on Audible.

Be forewarned, however: recording your own audio book isn't the super fun lark you may envision. The average audio book is 10 hours long and a serious mouthful to record. I recorded *Party Girl* over the course of three days, taking multiple breaks to gargle salt water or just rest my voice and complain in my head (since I was giving my voice a break) about how not fun the experience was.

Audible also has incredibly stringent audio standards and getting your audio files approved by them can take a very long time.

When it comes to releasing your audio book, you have two options: making it available at the same time as the print and ebook versions or having a second "launch" down the road. A second launch provides a nice opportunity to drum up renewed interest in your book and also gives you a cushion in case Audible doesn't approve your audio version by your deadline.

As for whether or not you want to record your book or use a narrator, make this decision with as unbiased a mind as your brain will allow. If you have no audio experience, your talents may be best left on the page.

If you decide to record it yourself, I want to emphasize what a good idea it is to do so when you're nearing the end of your line editing process so that you can catch errors.

And voila! Your book is ready to be released. What now?

Set Yourself Up for Success on Amazon

I'll be honest: I don't find uploading a book to Amazon to

be the easiest process. (Perhaps the best part of having a team is that I get to opt out of being the one to do this.)

First, it requires creating an author account on KDP (Kindle Direct Publishing), then selecting categories and keywords (more on that in a second) and then uploading your book and cover. As with Audible, the cover can get kicked back since Amazon's requirements are subject to change (though the re-approval process happens a trillion times faster than it does on Audible).

Selecting categories and keywords is more important than you may realize. As I mentioned in the Titles section, keywords allow readers to find your book when they're searching for information on your topic. Amazon allows you to pick up to six keywords and, as with search engine optimization, you can choose to either make each a word or a "long tail" keyword —otherwise known as a string of words or a phrase.

The best way I know of to determine which keywords to use is to get Publisher Rocket, a $97 software that allows you to search keywords and then see how many books out there are also using those keywords and even how much those authors are making. Selecting your own keywords using Publisher Rocket is therefore half art, half science: you want to use keywords that haven't been used by too many authors, but you also want them to be popular enough so that people can find your book and buy it.

Picking the right categories is even more important because this is when bestseller lists come into play. Amazon, as of now, only provides room on the back end for you to list the book in two categories. However, there's a handy work-around that is completely legit yet not widely known: you can contact Amazon and ask them to list the book in eight additional categories. This means that instead of your book having two opportunities to hit the bestseller list in its categories, it has 10.

Publisher Rocket is again your best friend when it comes to picking categories since it provides the same information for categories as it does for keywords. Just like with keywords, it's crucial that you use categories that fit your book; if you list your book in a category only because it seems to be netting great money for the authors who use it, but that category isn't right for your book, it's only going to annoy a reader.

Now that your book is out there, the next step is equal parts exhilarating and stressful...

Plan Your Launch

There's an endless array of ideas and strategies for having a successful launch so let me tell you the one we use at Launch Pad: the stealth release.

First, we tell the author to ask friends, acquaintances and fans to be a part of an Advanced Reader Team; we then give those team members a link to an electronic version of the book at least a month before launch. Through a series of emails we send out over that period, we nudge the team members to read the book and write a review.

Then, three days before the official release date, we instruct the group to purchase the ebook and then copy and paste their review. We price the book at $0.99 for those three days so we're not making anyone pay 10 bucks to do the author a favor. On release day, we change the ebook's price to $9.95 and announce the release to the world; this means that by the time readers see the book on Amazon, it already has a nice collection of positive reviews.

A word about your Advanced Reader Team: don't include your best friend, your mom or your spouse. Amazon has strict rules about which reviews they consider biased and will remove any they believe are written by someone too close to the author. This system is wildly arbitrary; an acquaintance of mine wrote a review of one of my books and received a notification that it was biased. However, I know people who have approved reviews written by their parents.

The ideal team members are people who support you but aren't in your inner circle. They're also people who have already purchased books in your genre. That's because the more those people have a history of buying books like yours, the more likely the "Customers Also Bought" algorithm is to kick in.

Also: Amazon has strict rules about authors paying anyone to review their books. You can thank all members with a gift but always encourage them to write honest and not necessarily rave reviews. I know I'm more likely to consider a book honestly reviewed if it has an array of different opinions and ratings than a book that has only 5-star raves.

Like I said, there are hundreds of other ways you can make a launch successful, including but not limited to: hiring a publicist to get media attention; preparing social media elements and swapping out every image you have on Instagram, Facebook, LinkedIn and anywhere else with pictures of your book and links to buy it; pinning links to the book to the top of all your social media; creating and posting cards with book quotes, blurbs and reviews; having launch events wherever you go (more on that in a bit); doing virtual book tours and making video trailers. And the list goes on.

Still, always remember: this is not just a launch. It's a journey. Your book can have a life as long as yours—or longer. The worst mistake you can make (I know because I made it over and over) is to move on from hyping your book after launch week. You've worked too hard for that.

Now that we've covered Amazon, let's talk about other places your book can be available.

Brainstorm Ways to Get in Bookstores

Remember how I said that the people I know who want to be published traditionally talk about their desire to have their book sold in stores for years? And remember how I broke down the harsh reality that that just doesn't happen most of the time?

This is where the author comes in. We list books in Ingram, which means that any bookstore can order the book. However, a store is unlikely to order a book customers aren't requesting. Our client Emily Lynn Paulson came up with a crafty work-around for this. She knew she wanted to do a book event in her hometown and happened to know one bookstore owner. When she asked the owner to carry her book and the store owner quickly agreed, Emily realized that other bookstores might be more open to carrying her book than she had initially realized.

She then reached out to the people on her Advanced Readers Team and to her social media followers, offering to give anyone who'd make the same request at their local bookstore a Starbucks gift card. Through her grassroots efforts, she was able to get her independently published book in over 70 bookstores around the country.

Many authors fantasize about having their book sold at airport bookstores, but get discouraged when they find out that it can cost up to $20,000. That inspired our client Darren Prince to get creative: when he was passing through an airport bookstore, he started chatting with one of the store clerks and asked if he could place his book there among the books for sale. Then he took some photos. Voila, it looked to his entire social media following like he'd made it to airport bookstores!

While we're on the subject of airports, let's talk about the part travel can play in your promotion.

Consider Touring

You know how I told you we're all unlikely, no matter who publishes us, to be handed an itinerary and have bookstores awaiting our arrival? That being said, there are countless other ways to go on tour.

While COVID19 changed travel forever, I believe it's worth highlighting authors who found ways to create tours for themselves.

I know a writer who decided to do a "couch tour": he reached out to readers and let them know that if any of them were willing to host a reading for him, he'd show up—books in tow. The move was so unique that *The New York Times* actually did a story about it—a story I saw, which inspired me to reach out and become one of the hosts.

I gathered a group of about 20 people and, after the reading, he sold us each a book. He did that dozens of times in different cities. This resulted in multiple book sales—and then there was the *Times* profile, which probably helped sell more copies than the entire tour put together. It pays to be creative.

Emily Lynn Paulson arranged for "mini launches" wherever she traveled during the months after her book came out. Even if she just held those events in her hotel room, she was able to gather people in those cities and towns to share and promote her book.

As a result of COVID19, virtual tours—meaning speaking to organizations and book clubs online—are only going to increase in popularity. One of the reasons they'll continue even after we're out of quarantine is that book stores realized during this pandemic just how successful virtual events could be (Book Passage in Marin held events with Anne Lamott, Dave Eggers and other household names; I participated in an online event with my local bookstore Book Soup). I consider this shift to virtual great news for those of us who aren't, say, Anne Lamott or Dave Eggers. If we have followers and subscribers all over the world, it's much easier to gather them online than to get them to fly out to our hometown to get a book signed. (That being said, at the time of this writing, in-store book events haven't resumed and I'm willing to brave any traffic for them as soon as they do.) This requires motivation and a lot of pitching but I know people who've had a lot of success with them.

Another option is to reach out to companies about bulk ordering copies of your book. My friend Ryan Hampton taught me this method when his first book was being released. He went through every contact in his address book, sifting out the people who worked for companies that might be interested in his book topic.

From there, he reached out with a tantalizing pitch: if the company or institution ordered bulk copies of his book, he would fly himself there to speak. He would also make that into an event local media would care about and reach out to local media himself. In short, he made his pitch an offer that a company would absolutely benefit from. By doing this, he sold thousands and thousands of copies. Of course, the same event could be held virtually.

To keep up with the meta-ness, I should tell you that I've done that with this book—and so you, dear reader, may be someone who got this book using this method.

At this point, you may be saying, "That's cool and all but I want to get on Ellen and Oprah! How can I make that happen?"

Educate Yourself About Traditional Media

The reality is that everyone wants to get Ellen and Oprah to promote their books and while your sales would indeed skyrocket if you could secure those spots, it's just not likely for most of us.

Also, most traditional media does not sell books. Back when *Party Girl* came out, I was told that if you could get your book in *People* magazine and on *The Today Show* in the same week, you were virtually guaranteed a bestseller.

That's simply not true today. And I don't have solid evidence that it was ever true. I got more press than I can even fully recall for *Party Girl*—and all the traditionally published books that followed—and yet I can name plenty of books that didn't have nearly as much press and sold more copies.

The reality is that the marketing rule of seven holds true for books. What this means is that usually a reader has to hear about your book seven times before they'll be motivated to buy. Seven appearances on *The Today Show* is no small feat.

It's far better to try to "own" rather than "rent" your audience. I'll get more into this in the next chapter, but for now, know that gathering potential readers and adding them to your email list is, in terms of book sales, worth so much more than any mainstream media you can get.

That being said, getting on TV shows and in magazines is undeniably cool. It's amazing social proof. You can add "as featured on/in" to your website along with the media icon. Other media outlets are more likely to consider you credible so each "hit" is likely to bring another. If you hire a publicist, just know that the quality of publicists, much like the quality of editors, varies greatly. If you want to take media matters into your own hands, I recommend subscribing to Help a Reporter Out (HARO); you'll start receiving three emails a day filled with requests from journalists looking for sources on every topic you can imagine.

When I subscribed to HARO, within a few days I saw a journalist who was looking for a source to talk about rehabs. I wrote him a two-line email introducing myself and he quoted me in the story he was writing for *Fortune* magazine. Since then he's quoted me in numerous other stories. That brief email I sent him, in other words, did for me more than publicists I'd paid obscene amounts of money had done.

Speaking of spending money...

Don't Be Afraid to Give Away Copies

If giving away copies of your book when you're hoping not to drop any more money on your book than you already have seems counter-intuitive, allow me to explain: you're probably not going to make money from book sales, but you can make a lot of money from having a book. In the next chapter, I'll get into different ways you can make money from your book but for now, know this: one book you give away can pay off 10 or 100-fold.

Think about it like this: if your book is related to your business, giving a copy of your book to a prospective client could cost you a few dollars and make you, depending on what you charge for your services, thousands and thousands of dollars. Earlier, I mentioned a client who released a book at the end of 2019. By early 2020, he told me that he'd added $500,000 to his bottom line. While he couldn't attribute the added income 100% to the book, every single new client he'd signed had read it. Unsurprisingly, we're now doing his second book.

The best way to give your book away is to simply carry it with you everywhere you go. Our client Darren always keeps copies in his suitcase so that whenever he travels, he can give away copies. That's how he was able to get in the airport bookstore! Our client Matt George saw a major athlete in a Vegas casino and was able to grab a photo with the athlete holding the book, which he then posted. But you don't have to limit your freebies to bold-faced names. You never know who will be impacted by your book or hire you as a result of it. I know people who leave copies of their books in their local Starbucks on the off-chance that a prospective client picks it up.

It's also probably worth the hassle and expense of sending copies out. Here's a tip I learned from business coach Alan Weiss: when sending a copy of your book to a prospective client, sign and send two. The person is then inclined to give the book to a friend (and if it's a prospective client, chances are that the prospective client is friends with other prospective clients), and people are much less likely to throw away a signed book.

Related: don't be afraid to shamelessly plug your book and the fact that you're an author wherever you can. Add "Bestselling Author" or "Author" to your email signature along with a link to the book. List that you're an author on your social media pages. Include it wherever you can. Why not? You worked hard for it, right? And you could call it selfish not to share your book with someone it could potentially help.

KEY TAKEAWAYS: The 19 Steps to Publishing Your Book

1) Educate Yourself About Traditional Publishing

2) Educate Yourself About Self and Hybrid Publishing

3) Come Up With Your Title

4) Rewrite

5) Hire an Editor

6) Consider Any Potential Legal Issues

7) Write Your Dedication and Acknowledgments

8) Gather Blurbs—and Possibly a Foreword

9) Come Up With Your Price

10) Get an ISBN

11) Have Your Cover Designed and Your Book Laid Out

12) Decide If You're Going to do a Hardcover

13) Decide If You're Going to do an Audio Book

14) Set Yourself Up for Success on Amazon

15) Plan Your Launch

16) Brainstorm Ways to Get in Bookstores

17) Consider Touring

18) Educate Yourself About Traditional Media

19) Don't Be Afraid to Give Away Copies

CHAPTER 13

Always Remember That *You're* The Messenger

NOW THAT WE'VE COVERED how to do a successful book launch, you need to get clear on what and how you want to do a book. Call this "expanding on your why."

For that, one factor matters more than any other.

You Need a Plan

Whether you want to use your book to create a coaching, consulting or other online business or to build an already existing business, the rules are the same: you need to get used to saying your message over and over again and you need to accept that some of what you'll try to do will not work overnight.

When I first decided I wanted to have a career I controlled, I thought creating online classes was the way to go. I bought courses by all the people who teach others how to become successful with online classes, studied them thoroughly, acquired all the software they recommended and spent months upon months creating and recording courses.

The webinars I did to sell them were nerve-wracking—somehow far more nerve-wracking than going live on CNN—and yet, they didn't work. I'd spend months creating and promoting a webinar only to have it sell a course or two.

I also tried coaching a group of students. I had an easier time signing people up for those programs, but it was still a struggle.

The day that one of the students in my coaching program told me she hated the program and found me useless, I had coffee with a new friend. I told him about this woman and how she had demanded a refund because my (quite inexpensive) program was too pricey. I then told him that people like Darren were asking me to publish their books.

He looked at me, a bit dumbfounded, and said, "You're telling me that you have wealthy people with abundant mentalities who treat you well and value your work and then you have people without abundant mentalities telling you that you're worthless and that you're putting your effort into the latter?"

I nodded. I hadn't realized it until that moment.

From that day forward, I switched my focus from the latter group to the former and that's when business started booming. That is officially when I created my new playing field.

While I still coach students and make comparatively little money doing it, the fact that I'm not dependent on their payments for my income means I only allow people into the program who I sense have abundant mentalities, no matter what they can afford to pay.

A few months into coaching my current group of students, I realized something else: what I was learning from working with them was giving me invaluable insight into what my audience wanted. I've now set up a certification program so that those who work with me can spread the Launch Pad method to even more people.

Coaching students also gives me unbelievable support. Whether I'm asking if they'll review or comment on something or read one of my books, this small but mighty group shows up with a passion that almost makes me cry. And that brings me to something else.

You Need a Small But Mighty Group

We've already talked about how you need an audience. It's going to start small, just like it will for anyone whose last name doesn't start with "Kardash." But you need them as much as you need your message.

So how do you get them?

I have a course on how to build an audience, and its main message is this: it takes way longer than you might think so you better make it fun.

Building an Audience 1: Instagram

Let's first talk about the platform I've found to be most effective: Instagram.

No, Instagram is not just for mindless scrolling, followed by Ben & Jerry's-accompanied sessions of comparing and despairing. Some of my biggest clients have come from Instagram, including my first client Darren, who found me from doing a hashtag search for recovery.

I resisted IG for so long, telling myself I was a words person; the resistance just meant I was late to the party. Still,

Instagram is not a requirement for everyone. I know people with companies that pull in millions who wouldn't know how to sign onto Instagram and I know people with millions of followers who don't make a penny. If you're in the former category, ignore this. If you're not, here's what I suggest:

Figure out your message: Sound familiar? Well, Instagram is an amazing place to hone and perfect whatever it is you have to tell the world. If you're thinking, "I have more than one message," great. Now pick the one you believe in most passionately and that you also believe could eventually net you the highest income. The message I always try to convey through Instagram is "share your story" and I sprinkle that in most posts. Your message could be "recovery is possible" or "self-love is everything" or any damn thing you want. Just know what it is so you can share it.

Don't *only* share your message: Before you go calling me a hypocrite, know this: people are much more likely to care about your "thing" if they know you. So share yourself—your pets, your significant other, your penchant for karaoke, whatever the hell makes you you. I recommend peppering in some personal material every three or four posts.

Be consistent: As a non-psychic who doesn't work at Instagram, I can't tell you how the algorithm works. But I can tell you that it favors people who use the app the most. This doesn't mean you have to post multiple times a day but if you want to grow, I would aim to post at least three times a week. You can go crazy using different apps to try to determine what time of day is best for you, like I did for a short time, but you can probably just observe when your posts tend to get the most interaction and determine when and what to post from there.

Be brave: I'll be honest: I feel unbelievably vain posting photo after photo of myself and the people who unfollow me every week (I tend to get as many unfollows as follows, therefore remaining at a steady 20,000-ish followers) surely agree. But I do it not only because I *am* unbelievably vain but also because it works. Yes, my boyfriend is tired of taking 20 photos of me in a certain pose so that I can pick the one I believe is most Insta-worthy but if it's going to net me a $50,000 client, I'm going to continue to do it. And I don't take it nearly as far as others do. A woman I know who has millions of Instagram followers says to really grow on the platform, you have to be polarizing. You have to, she says, be willing to have people hate you. Since I'm a fragile flower who doesn't think inspiring hatred would be worth it even if it made my audience grow, I resist this method. I just post what allows me to feel honest while still honoring my own privacy. Speaking of which…

Post what feels honest: In case it's not obvious, the captions we post are just as, if not more, important than the photos. I used to judge people who used all 2200 characters until I had the experience of posting blogs on Medium that no one read, then re-posting the same content on Instagram and getting an amazing response. Instagram, for better or worse, is where people are consuming content these days and while a picture may be worth a thousand words, it's far easier to convey your message through the words you put below your photos.

Talk to your people: While it can be easy to get caught up in numbers, never forget that every single person who's following you made the choice to follow you. How nice is that? You may choose to follow them back or you may choose not to but if someone comments, make your best effort to respond to that comment. Not only do more comments show the Instagram algorithm that followers are responding to your post, but it also shows people you value them.

Stay on message: If you're trying to build a business, don't post bikini photos. That may be obvious but I can name a handful of people who claim to want the former but do the latter. I get it; for certain people, a bikini photo is going to get a lot more likes than an inspiring business quote, but staying on message and building your story is so much more important than the validation that comes from those likes.

Use the features: Instagram is constantly busting out new features and the algorithm allegedly loves to favor those who use them. Stories are those short videos and photos you can post by pressing on your image in the top left corner. If you have over 10,000 followers, you have a "swipe up" option, which means that users can actually click on a link you provide. (A standard Instagram caption doesn't allow for clickable links.) You can also "go live" on Instagram, adding other people to chat with or interview. For longer videos, you can use IGTV.

Building an Audience 2: Emails

Make no mistake: starting and maintaining an email list is no small feat. It requires dedication and persistence. It is also the best way there is to build an audience. So how do you do it?

Sign up for an email provider account: There are countless companies that offer this service—from Mailchimp to Constant Contact to Drip to Kajabi (what I use and love). Most of us start out on Mailchimp, not only because they offer free accounts but also because it's the simplest. Once your list grows and you want to start doing more advanced things, like segmenting which people purchase certain offers or click on certain things, you can move on to one of the others.

Come up with a lead magnet: Once you have an email provider, you need something to incentivize people to sign up for your list. Whether it's a quiz or a 10-step guide or anything else, create a PDF that's valuable to your ideal newsletter subscriber. Just putting SIGN UP FOR MY LIST on your site is unlikely to get the sort of traction that SIGN UP FOR MY AWESOME THING THAT YOU FOR SURE WANT will. Settling on the right lead magnet isn't easy; I've probably tried out a dozen and while some have worked well, I've never had one that was a gusher that inspired thousands of people to sign up for my list. It really is one email address at a time.

Craft a nurture sequence: Once someone's on your list, they may not have a clue who you are. That's why it's a good idea to warm them up to you. Set up a series of emails that go out every few days, starting the minute they sign up, slowly explaining who you are and what you do or offer. It's ideal to provide a great deal of value in those emails, whether it's providing another free download, links to your most popular blog posts or special offers on something you sell.

Write your subscribers! This may seem obvious but you need to communicate with your subscribers regularly—ideally once a week. Just think about when you receive an email from some company you don't even remember. "Delete" followed by "unsubscribe," am I right? Try to provide your audience with information, stories or links every week so that they'll want to open your emails. If writing them every week seems laborious, consider this: it's going to get easier the longer you do it. Also: you're a writer! So this is good practice, right? Plus, this is the beginning of your 1000 true fan base so it's worth it.

Track what works: Once you're committed to writing your subscribers, start looking at what they like. Check out your open rates and try not to get discouraged. The average open rate is between 15-25%; if I get over 30%, I'm giddy. Experiment with different subject lines. The highest open rate I ever got was for an email with the subject line "Oops!" (I had just sent a different one by mistake so I was telling subscribers not to open that one.) My second most popular was "Can you help me?"

Conclusion: subscribers like mistakes. They also like to help. They don't like to be marketed to. A successful copywriter I know recommends crafting subject lines that sound like an email from Mom; the example she gives is "dinner on Sunday?"

KEY TAKEAWAYS:
How to Build an Audience

8 Tips for Mastering Instagram:

1) Figure out your message

2) Don't only share your message

3) Be consistent

4) Be brave

5) Post what feels honest

6) Talk to your people

7) Stay on message

8) Use the features

5 Steps to Successful Newsletters:

1) Sign up for an email provider account

2) Come up with a lead magnet

3) Craft a nurture sequence

4) Write your subscribers

5) Track what works

CHAPTER 14

The Best Ways to Make Your Book Successful

W HILE THE PREVIOUS CHAPTER focused on the three biggies when it comes to audience building, there are myriad other ways to focus more specifically on launching a book. These strategies are so important that they're the focus of my podcast, Launch Pad.

On the show, I interview *New York Times* bestselling authors, expert marketers who only do books to grow their careers and everyone in between. If you're interested in delving into the topic, I highly recommend subscribing to the show. Here are some of the best tips and techniques that experts have shared with me.

Annabelle Gurwitch

Annabelle Gurwitch is an actress, activist, and the author of *The New York Times* bestseller and Thurber Prize finalist *I See You Made an Effort*. Her other books include: *Wherever You Go, There They Are* and *You Say Tomato, I Say Shut Up* (co-authored with Jeff Kahn).

She was the co-host of *Dinner and a Movie* on TBS and has appeared on NPR, *The Today Show, CBS Early Show, Real Time with Bill Maher,* PBS and numerous CNN and MSNBC programs. Her essays and satire have been featured in *The New Yorker, The New York Times, The Wall Street Journal, The Los Angeles Times, AARP, Real Simple, Prevention,* The Los Angeles Book Review, The Daily Beast and Time.com, among other media outlets.

Her top three book launch tips are:

1) Organize your book around a topic people are already talking about. "I don't need to invent an audience for something that's in the social zeitgeist," she told me. "I just need to identify where people are already talking about the thing that I'm doing."

2) Contact media that has supported similar books. "I looked at which media was giving *Transparent* press, not because my work was related to Jill Soloway's work but because Jill is also a Jewish artist."

3) Schedule live events by reaching out to organizers, telling them you'll be in the area (whether you will be or not) and then, when they accept you, piggy back other events around it. "I will reach out to people and say, 'Hey, I've got a book coming out. I'm going to be in your area,' whether I will be in that area or not. Then I'm able to contact or tell the team of people I'm working with, 'I'm going to be in Boston speaking at this women's conference at the time of the book release. Is there a book festival that's happening then?'"

Courtney Friel

Courtney Friel is the author of the #1 bestselling book, *Tonight at 10: Kicking Booze and Breaking News*. She's best known for her work as a news anchor at KTLA in Los Angeles, where she also hosts the video podcast "Keepin' It Friel: Conversations on Recovery." She previously worked as a national correspondent for Fox News Channel and hosted the "World Poker Tour."

Her top three book launch tips are:

1) Avoid traditional publishing. "People don't get that it's a countdown to heartbreak. Even if it works out, it's this crazy time and money investment that rarely works out. I tried selling this book to a traditional publisher and all that means is I wasted a lot of time and money on a proposal that didn't sell."

2) Save some money so you can spend it on your launch. "The best way to invest is to plan travel and then make the most of whatever you can do to promote your book. Maybe you can have an event or get on local media."

3) Find the news hook in your story. "If your book is about a school shooting, you need to be listening to the news to hear if there's a school shooting. If you're writing a book about cars and you see on ABC there's the guy that does the car segments, look for him—on social media or wherever. You've got to be like a little Nancy Drew."

Dave Chesson

Dave Chesson is the founder of Kindlepreneur.com, a website devoted to teaching advanced book marketing, and the creator of Publisher Rocket software. He's worked with authors such as Orson Scott Card and Ted Dekker and his tactics help both fiction and non-fiction authors at all levels get their books discovered by the right readers.

His top three book launch tips are:

1) When you start writing your book, build relationships with people who can ultimately support you—influencers, other authors and the like. "The day you decide to put finger to keyboard and hit that first key is the day you need to start marketing," he told me. "Start building relationships with other people—either your target market or other authors in the area. Don't just go up to them when your book's coming out and say, 'Hey, you're a really great author! Hey, would you mind promoting my book?'"

2) Build a course that you promote with your book. "I helped Pat Flynn with the launch of *Will It Fly?* and he put a link to a free course at the front of the book," Dave said. "He said that one third of book buyers signed up for the free course. Then he created a paid course and the day he launched that paid course, he made over $111,000 just using the email list that he built from his readers."

3) Don't be afraid to encourage your readers to write good reviews. "I will write at the end of the book about what brought me to the point of starting the book and the fears that came from it—just reminding them that the words came from a human being," he revealed. "So, I'll tell a bit of my journey and what I had to go through to get this thing created for them. And then I'll remind them how important book reviews are. Authors understand it, but readers forget how important good reviews are and how much bad reviews hurt. And so I'll let them know how important that review is for me and that I will be there to read each and every one of them."

Jane Ubell-Meyer

Jane Ubell-Meyer is an award-winning entrepreneur and former television and film producer. Her TV credits include *Good Morning America* and *Entertainment Tonight*, among many others. She taught at New York's Fashion Institute of Technology for seven years and is a speaker and mentor to authors and entrepreneurs. These days, she runs Bedside Reading, a program that places books in the bedrooms of luxury hotels and in the media. She's also one of the most out-of-the-box thinkers I've ever met when it comes to book promotion.

Her top three book launch tips are:

1) Find a unique sponsor. She said, "Let's say your book takes place in Detroit. Go to the Detroit Tourism Board and tell them, 'Hey, I just wrote a book. It takes place in Detroit. Can you give me a launch party?'

Think 'Are there any marketing dollars from the city of Detroit for artists working in Detroit promoting the city of Detroit?' A lot of businesses, even Home Depot, have discretionary funds to help local people in the community."

2) Layer your marketing and promotion. "Don't look at it as 'one and done,'" she cautioned. "Hit every medium—print, blogs, podcasts, and radio—over an extended period of time. Everyone makes a big deal about the launch because they want to become a bestseller. Your book should have a life for many years."

3) Make your cover amazing. "A cover can repel or attract. I have said to people, 'Yeah, what a great concept. Great book. What if you redo the cover?' They'll say, 'Oh, I love the cover. You know, my friend did the artwork and blah, blah blah.' And I say, 'It doesn't matter. Do you want readers or not?'"

These are just a few of the many tips revealed in my podcast. I could fill a whole book with them. To listen to the rest, subscribe to the show.

KEY TAKEAWAYS: The 12 Best Ways to Make Your Launch Successful

1) Organize your book around a topic people are already talking about

2) Contact media that has supported similar books

3) Schedule live events by reaching out to organizers, telling them you'll be in the area (whether you will be or not) and then, when they accept you, piggy back other events around it

4) Avoid traditional publishing

5) Save some money so you can spend it on your launch

6) Find the news hook in your story

7) Build relationships with people who can ultimately support you—influencers, other authors and the like

8) Create a course that you promote in your book

9) Encourage your readers to write good reviews

10) Find a unique sponsor

12) Make your cover amazing

Making Your Message Your Business

O KAY, ELEVATOR RIDERS, WE'VE made it to the end. We've analyzed our messes, determined our messages and come up with a plan for sharing it with the world. There's just one last fact I'd like to reinforce: while few of us will make a considerable amount of money from our book sales, it is wholly possible to create a successful business from a book.

Of course building a business—and finding clients for that business—isn't easy. I know that in order to make and keep the business successful, I have to do…well, a lot.

I have to get clear about where I believe my ideal clients are and start showing up there—whether it's a pricey marketing conference, an out-of-city workshop or a dinner party. I then have to prove to them that I, out of all the people out there offering my service, am the one to hire. And I have to accept that some of those people might still meet me, be familiar with my work and hire someone else.

I have to study other businesses as if I were in business school—subscribing to their newsletters, attending their webinars, combing through their blog posts and websites, listening to their podcasts—so that I can always be coming up with new ideas about what clients want.

I have to be indefatigable when it comes to my marketing—consistently updating my website, my offerings, my blog posts, my podcast, my newsletters and everything else. I have to be reading marketing books, experimenting with Facebook ads and embracing my business with the same enthusiasm I put toward my writing.

I have to manage people—something that can be challenging, not only because my character defects pop up but also because anyone I manage is bringing to me whatever issues they have with authority. And so I have to learn not to take it personally when they're disgruntled—and to be open to seeing when their issues mean I have to change something about the company—or myself.

I have to consistently be observing the way we work—and always looking to refine and improve it. I have to constantly focus on trying to make our clients feel as special and taken care of as I felt un-special and disregarded when I was in the traditional publishing game.

I have to be tireless when it comes to sharing my belief that everyone who feels they have a story to share should publish a book—and that their book can help their bottom line.

I have to do all sorts of tasks I'd rather not do—from negotiating deals with clients to being the bad guy if they don't pay on time. But perhaps the hardest part is that I have to live with the pressure of everything resting on my shoulders. The work I do, as I see it, isn't only producing the book; it's taking on the emotional and literal responsibility of making clients' dreams come true. (I'm not being dramatic here; *The New York Times* reported in 2002 that 81% of people dream of writing a book and from my unscientific surveys, I would guess that the percentage is even higher today.)

For all the toil, the rewards of running a business are almost impossible to describe. I get to make the sort of living I never could have imagined back when I was being published by HarperCollins. More importantly, I get to facilitate a process that can change people's lives. I'm the one who controls the elevator so if I ever feel stuck on a floor, I have all the tools I need to fix that.

But, of course, no one's going to just hand you a business. You have to work tirelessly until it clicks. In my experience, the transition from having expertise to being able to use that expertise to run a business happens, as Hemingway put it, gradually and then suddenly.

Still, there are all sorts of "indie" business opportunities you can experiment with in the meantime. In Chapter 13, I suggested you come up with an after-book plan, whether it's building a coaching business, becoming a consultant, launching a speaking career or anything else.

So consider where you've put your sweat equity; it's probably a skill you could both put into a business and would find rewarding.

You could try to get a spokesperson deal. The best way to start is to leverage the relationships you already have. Look at the people you know through a new lens...a lens through which you can support one another in your respective goals—the way Darren Prince did when he landed the six-figure spokesperson deal. The person who hired him did so because Darren, thanks to his book, had become a valuable asset.

If you're thinking, "Well, I'm not a sports agent and so I

don't know people who can hire me for fancy spokesperson deals," I encourage you to make a list of the people you know; go through your address book, look at Facebook, do whatever you need to do in order to inspire your brain to look beyond the obvious. Then ask yourself: who do I know who knows other people who I may be able to work with? Keep going from there.

If public speaking is your goal, brainstorm a list of organizations that might hire you as a speaker and then, if you get hired, figure out how to make your visit into a news event the way Ryan Hampton did. Of course, it isn't as simple as publishing a book and waiting for the speaking offers to roll in. While we have a course on the exact steps to take to launch a speaking career, the most important fact to keep in mind is that it can be a slow build.

Still, speaking is one of those careers where your fee can skyrocket once you have success. Some authors who are currently making a killing on the speaking circuit are Doris Kearns Goodwin, who nets $40K a gig, and Tim Ferriss and Malcolm Gladwell, who are each in the $50K-plus range. I get a mere $3000-$5000 for a speaking gig, which is great since speaking isn't a priority for me, but it's pennies compared to these others!

If you want to develop a coaching program, take the material in your book and think about how you can develop it into material you could teach. With a program, you'll be able to help people on a much deeper level than you did with your book while also taking a deeper dive into the topic yourself. Who knows! It might even provide you with enough material for book two!

If you want to take coaching to the next level (and possibly get paid better for it), consider offering consulting services to companies that could use whatever expertise you established with the book.

You could also create a certification program by training other people in what you've been teaching since the best preparation for developing a curriculum and providing certification is having a coaching program.

You could create a subscription or monthly membership program—with videos and worksheets you've created, guest interviews, in-person events or daily or weekly video check-ins. The main factor to remember with membership programs is that success is defined by how much direct involvement you offer.

You could put on events. We're living in the day and age of event throwing and your event can be anything from a workshop to a retreat to a weekly gathering. It can be held at a cafe, a theater, a holistic health center or an AirBnB. (I've held events at all of these places.) Your agenda can cover the same material as your monthly programs. But here's the truth: people are often just aching to connect with a like-minded community and thus the activities matter far less than the simple fact that the event is happening.

You could create a mastermind. If you look at who runs the biggest mastermind groups—people like Joe Polish, Brendon Burchard, Jeff Walker and Russell Brunson—you'll notice that they're all authors.

You could sell a physical product. James Swanwick, the author of *The 30-Day No Alcohol Challenge: Your Simple Guide to Easily Reduce Or Quit Alcohol*, watched his career skyrocket when he expanded his expertise from "quitting drinking" to "lifestyle" and started selling blue blocking glasses.

Finally, you could launch a podcast. Yes, there are a billion podcasts out there. But anyone who tells you it's too late to start one is lying (see what I have to say on the topic here). If you're looking for the next steps to get started, consider taking my free class on it. One factor to keep in mind: podcasts are very rarely a source of revenue; much like a book, they are a credibility builder, but they are even better at providing an opportunity for people to develop a "know, like and trust" factor with you and therefore they support all your other endeavors. And if you have ANY of the offerings above, your podcast will absolutely bring in clients.

Before you get overwhelmed by these options, remember that the first step is to write and publish your book. While my company is here to help with that, you may not need us. And so let me leave you with a thought you perhaps want to pass along to your future readers: you got this.

I'll see you on the top floor.

If this book helped you in any way, I'd be so grateful if you would share that with others in the form of a review. Once you put your own story out there, you'll discover how much these reviews mean. Think of your review as paying it forward but without the earnestness of that Haley Joel Osment movie.

Just a reminder: if you want to begin work on your own memoir, I highly recommend downloading my one-page memoir structure cheat sheet, which you can get by going to www.messdownload.com.

KEY TAKEAWAYS:
How to Use Your Book to Grow Your Career

6 Steps to Making Your Memoir Your Business:

1) Figure out where your ideal clients are—and go there

2) Study other businesses as if you're in business school

3) Be indefatigable when it comes to marketing

4) Learn to manage people and consistently analyze the way you work

5) Be tireless when it comes to sharing your message

6) Become willing to do what you don't want to

9 Opportunities to Pursue as an Author:

1) Go after spokesperson jobs

2) Get speaking gigs

3) Start a coaching program

4) Create a certification program

5) Offer a membership group

6) Throw events

7) Launch a mastermind

8) Sell physical products

9) Create a podcast

Acknowledgments

WHILE THE WRITING OF this book went relatively quickly, the lessons I needed to learn in order to write it took, well, my entire life.

The transition I describe, from broken girl to functional woman, wouldn't have been possible if I hadn't been lucky enough to fall into the loving embrace of the Log Cabin in West Hollywood 20 years ago, where I found the acceptance I'd always craved from a host of people too insane (in the best ways) and numerous to list. Anadel Barbour and Lyra Barrera then helped me face the un-faceable with more support and brilliance than I could have imagined possible. And without the guidance of Joe Polish and everyone I've met through Genius Network, I would never have been able to create, let alone run, a thriving business.

Thank you to Lisa Smith, Natali Morris and Caitlin Scanlon for reading this manuscript and giving me feedback. Thank you to the team who helped with the audio book, most especially Jim Agnew—who also happens to be the world's best boyfriend. Thank you to the Launch Pad crew—cover designer, Onur Aksoy, for doing revision after revision until it was perfect; project manager Ryan Aliapoulios whose patience and talent knows no bounds; and my brother from another mother, Ryan Hampton, for helping to spread the word. Thank you to Rajesh Setty for coming up with the term "biz-oir" and Parsifal Tritsch for his incredibly creative promotion ideas. Thank you to Emily Redondo for manning the Advanced Reader team; my Elite Messengers Jeff Kober, Catherine Just, Korey Pollard and Corrine Casanova and everyone from the Inner Circle and beyond who supported this book along the way.

I'm incredibly grateful to the Launch Pad team, which includes, in addition to the Ryans, Kristen McGuiness, Swan Huntley, Becky Sasso, Heather Mize and all the freelancers who've helped us to grow. And the business wouldn't exist at all without clients who have given us at least as much as we've given them—including Darren Prince, Emily Lynn Paulson, Tim Conn, Gene Moran, Matt George, Joe Gorga, Courtney Friel, Alexis Haines and so many others. Thank you as well to the incredible authors who have shared their expertise with me on my podcast and the coaching students who have allowed me a front row seat on their journey. It's been an honor to help you bring your stories into the world.

Also by Anna David

Party Girl

How to Get Successful By F*cking Up Your Life

The Miracle Morning for Addiction Recovery
(with Hal Elrod and Joe Polish)

For other books by Anna David, go to annadavid.com/books

Find Anna:

Instagram.com/annabdavid
Facebook.com/annabdavid
YouTube.com/user/overannalyze